the HAIRY BIKERS'

12 Days of Christmas

the
HAIRY BIKERS'
12 Days of
Christmas

WEIDENFELD & NICOLSON

Our dedications

Dave: To Dr David, Jane, Amy, Sian and Calum Easton, not forgetting the wonderful Phyllis and Claire. Thanks for the amazing Christmases we've spent together.

Si: To Margaret Dodd, my mother-in-law and queen of soup and a sandwich.

First published in hardback in Great Britain in 2010 by
Weidenfeld & Nicolson, an imprint of the Orion Publishing Group Ltd
Orion House, 5 Upper St Martin's Lane, London WC2H 9EA
an Hachette UK Company

10 9 8 7 6 5 4 3 2 1

A CIP catalogue record for this book is available from the British Library.

ISBN: 978-0-297-86027-3

Photography by Cristian Barnett
Food styling by Sammy-Jo Squire
Design by Kate Barr
Edited by Jinny Johnson
Proofread by Elise See Tai
Index by Elizabeth Wiggans

Printed and bound in Germany

The Orion Publishing Group's policy is to use papers that are natural, renewable and recyclable and made from wood grown in sustainable forests. The logging and manufacturing processes are expected to conform to the environmental regulations of the country of origin.

www.orionbooks.co.uk

Hey folks – Happy Christmas!

This is our favourite time of year and what better way to celebrate than to cook fab festive food for the people you love.

In this book we share our favourite dishes for the Christmas season – some much-loved traditional recipes such as mince pies and Christmas pud, all tried and trusted stalwarts, as well as lots of new ideas that we hope will become part of your festive feasts. Have a go at our Christmas panna cotta and our cranberry, macadamia and butterscotch Christmas pudding – they're out of this world!

Of course, Christmas isn't just one day, so we've come up with all sorts of tasty dishes for Christmas Eve, Boxing Day, New Year's Eve and Twelfth Night, not to mention weekends and extra bank holidays. There are cheeky cocktails to tame your in-laws, ingenious recipes for all those leftovers – try our goose risotto, turkey curry, and turkey and ham pie – and fancy snacks to nibble on in front of the telly. And we've included expert advice on turkeys, Christmas drinks and putting together a cheeseboard, as well as our very own Christmas Countdown to help you get the perfect dinner on the table and stay smiling.

We want to help you make this year's Christmas your best and most relaxed ever and we hope that our very own Hairy Christmas cookbook will be just the companion you need during all the festive celebrations.

A big Christmas hug

Getting
ahead

TRADITIONAL GRAVLAX
WITH DILL & MUSTARD SAUCE

This traditional version of gravlax keeps very well in the fridge for up to five days once made.
Serve on rye bread for canapés or as starter with salad and perhaps a few prawns.

SERVES 16

2 sides of salmon,
about 750g each, pin bones removed
75g sea salt flakes
50g soft light brown sugar
40g fresh dill, stalks discarded and
fronds finely chopped
1 tbsp coarsely ground black pepper
rye bread, to serve

DILL & MUSTARD SAUCE
3 large free-range egg yolks
2 tbsp white wine vinegar
2 tbsp Dijon mustard
1 tbsp caster sugar
½ tsp sea salt flakes
freshly ground black pepper to taste
300ml sunflower oil
20g fresh dill, stalks discarded and fronds
finely chopped

Wipe the salmon and check that all the little pin bones have been removed (see page 10). Place one side of salmon in a long, ceramic dish, skin side down. The dish should be large enough to hold the salmon without it curling and deep enough to catch any juices that are released during the curing process.

Mix the sea salt, sugar, dill and pepper in a bowl and sprinkle the mixture evenly over the fish. Place the other piece of salmon on top, skin side up. Cover the fish with a couple of sheets of clingfilm and place a tray or a slightly smaller baking tin on top. Weigh down with several cans of beans or some old-fashioned kitchen scale weights.

Place the salmon in the fridge and leave for 3 nights – make sure the temperature stays at 5°C or just under. Every day, remove the fish from the fridge. Turn it over, cover with new clingfilm, weigh it down and return it to the fridge to continue curing.

When ready to serve, transfer the salmon to a clean board and discard the curing liquid. Pat the fish dry with kitchen paper. Some people scrape or rinse off the dill marinade, but you don't have to. Slice the salmon from the tail end in thin, almost horizontal pieces. Arrange on plates with crustless rye bread and top with spoonfuls of the dill and mustard sauce to serve.

DILL & MUSTARD SAUCE
Put the egg yolks, vinegar, mustard and sugar in a food processor and season with salt and black pepper. Blitz until smooth, then gradually add the oil, with the motor still running, and blend until the sauce is smooth and thick. Add 3–4 tablespoons of cold water and blend for a few seconds more until the mixture has a soft, dropping consistency. Adjust the seasoning to taste, add the dill to the sauce and blend quickly until just combined. Transfer to a bowl. The sauce will keep for 3 days in the fridge.

Any leftover salmon can be frozen. Wrap it really well in a freezer bag, squeezing out as much air as possible, and freeze for up to a month. If you slice the salmon while it's still frozen, you'll be able to make the slices even thinner.

CHRISTMAS GRAVLAX
WITH DILL, TREACLE & CUMIN

This is our festive take on the traditional Swedish gravlax. It is raw salmon cured with salt, sugar and dill in the traditional way, but we also use cumin and treacle in the mix. This gives it a sensational flavour that we think makes it extra Christmassy. Serve with a green salad and traditional dill sauce (see page 10) or simply with a squeeze of lemon – just the job for Christmas dinner.

SERVES 16

2 sides of salmon,
about 750g each, pin bones removed
100g sea salt flakes
100g caster sugar
1 tbsp crushed white peppercorns
a large bunch of fresh dill,
finely chopped
2 tbsp treacle
2 tbsp ground cumin
extra sea salt flakes

While making gravlax, keep your hands, chopping boards and any utensils as clean and hygienic as possible. Wipe the fish fillets and place them on a large, clean board. Make sure all the pin bones have been removed by running your finger down the centre of the salmon. If you feel any little bones, ease them out with tweezers – or we sometimes use a pair of pliers!

Mix together the sea salt, sugar, peppercorns, dill, treacle and cumin in a bowl to make the curing mixture. At this stage it will look like a bowl of black gravel.

Sprinkle a layer of the extra salt on a large piece of foil and place one salmon fillet on top, skin side down. Cover the flesh with the curing mixture. Place the other piece of salmon skin side up on top and scatter over some more sea salt flakes.

Wrap the salmon up carefully and seal the edges of the foil to make a tight parcel. We always wrap it in another piece of foil to help the seal. Put the parcel on a baking tray and put a plate and a weight on the top to apply pressure to the parcel. We use several cans of beans or some kitchen scale weights.

Place the salmon in the fridge and leave it to cure for at least 2 days. Turn the parcel twice a day so the juices from the top and bottom half drain evenly. Juice will escape through the parcel so when you turn the salmon, discard any excess liquid – this is part of the curing process as the salt draws the moisture out of the fish. You can leave the fish another day if you want.

Unwrap the parcel and discard the bits of dill and peppercorn. The gravlax is now ready to eat. Cut the slices on the bias so you get slices that show off the black edges made by the treacle. Wrap the remaining salmon in clingfilm and refrigerate. This needs eating within a week but that shouldn't be a problem!

PICKLED PEARS

This is a proper Christmas pickle, inspired by a meeting in a car park with the godfather himself, Antonio Carluccio. Make these, and pickled onions, to give as presents.

**MAKES ENOUGH FOR
2 x 1.5 LITRE JARS**

20 conference pears
1 litre white wine vinegar
500g caster sugar
3 star anise
1 large stick of cinnamon, broken into 4 pieces
1 tbsp allspice berries
½ tsp cloves
1 dsrtsp juniper berries
peel of 1 lemon, removed in thin curls with a potato peeler
3 sprigs of rosemary

Peel the pears carefully, leaving the stalks intact. Pour the vinegar into a large, non-reactive saucepan (stainless steel, glass and ceramic pans don't react with acids like copper and aluminium do). Add the sugar, spices, lemon peel, rosemary and 500ml of water. Bring to the boil, then add the pears. Cover the pan and gently simmer the pears for 10–15 minutes until they are tender. Remove the pears and set them aside, then boil the poaching liquid for 5 minutes until it is reduced to intensify the flavour.

Divide the pears between the sterilised jars and pour half the liquid into each one. Try to make sure each jar has an even amount of spices. Seal tightly and store. You can keep these for a couple of months, but they will be good to eat after a week. Once a jar has been opened, keep it in the fridge and eat the pears within 2 weeks.

PICKLED ONIONS

MAKES 1 LARGE JAR

500g salt (you can use low-sodium salt)
1kg pickling onions or small shallots
1 litre malt vinegar (or try cider or white wine vinegar if you're feeling flush)
1 tbsp pickling spices
2 bay leaves
1 stick of cinnamon
1 star anise
1 sprig of thyme

Boil 2 litres of water, add the salt and stir until the salt has dissolved. Set aside to cool. Peel the onions, leaving the roots intact so the onions don't fall apart. Put them in a bowl and cover with the cooled salty water (brine). Place a plate on the top to keep the onions in the liquid and leave in the fridge for 24 hours to allow the brine to draw the water out of the onions.

Pour the vinegar into a non-reactive pan (see above). Bring to a simmer, then remove from the heat and add the spices, bay leaves, cinnamon, star anise and thyme. The hot vinegar will draw out the flavours. Leave to cool completely.

Rinse the brined onions in cold water and pat them dry with kitchen paper. Pack the onions tightly into a sterilised jar, cover with the spiced vinegar and seal tightly. Use greaseproof circles to cover the tops if the jars have metal lids or the vinegar will rot the lids. Leave the onions for at least a fortnight for the flavours to develop – a couple of months is even better.

TRADITIONAL CHRISTMAS PUDDING

This is our version of the classic pud and very good it is too. You can make it up to six months before Christmas if you like, then just cover it with fresh baking parchment and keep in a cool, dry cupboard. To make the pud extra rich and moist, top it up with a splash of brandy every week.

SERVES 6–8

100g wholemeal breadcrumbs
120ml beer, preferably stout such as Guinness
2 free-range eggs, beaten
100ml sunflower oil
100g brown sugar
120g wholemeal flour
50g almonds, skinned and finely chopped
4 tsp mixed spice, or to taste
½ tsp grated nutmeg
200g raisins
300g sultanas
zest of 1 lemon and 1 orange
1 tsp salt
50g cooking apple, chopped
50g orange segments, chopped

Tip the breadcrumbs into a large mixing bowl, add the stout and leave them to soak for a few minutes while you get the rest of the ingredients together.

Add the eggs, sunflower oil and sugar to the bowl and mix until well combined. Then add the remaining ingredients, except the apple and orange segments, and stir for about 5 minutes, or until the mixture is sticky and everything is thoroughly mixed together. Add the chopped apple and orange and stir them in well.

Grease a 1.2 litre pudding basin with butter and spoon in the Christmas pudding mixture. Cover with a double piece of greaseproof paper and a single piece of foil, then secure with string. Place the bowl on an upturned heatproof saucer or small trivet in a large, deep saucepan and add enough just-boiled water to come halfway up the sides of the basin. Cover the pan with a tight-fitting lid, place over a low heat and steam the pud in the simmering water for 6 hours. Check regularly and top up with boiling water as necessary.

Once the pud is steamed, allow it to cool before wrapping and storing it away until Christmas. Or, if you want a really trad look for a pudding to give as a present, wrap it in muslin.

On the big day, steam the pud again for 2 hours and serve with one of our delicious sauces (see page 120).

CHRISTMAS CAKE

Take it from us – this is the best. If you can't find barley malt syrup or brown rice syrup you could use molasses and normal golden syrup. You can make this cake up to six weeks before Christmas.

MAKES A 20CM SQUARE OR 23CM ROUND CAKE

150ml sunflower oil, plus extra for greasing the tin
280g plain flour
650g sultanas
300g raisins
20g dates, chopped
1 tsp bicarbonate of soda
1 tsp salt
1 tsp ground cardamom
1 tsp mixed spice
120ml barley malt syrup (or molasses)
180g brown rice syrup (or golden syrup)
4 free-range eggs, beaten
20g dried pineapple (rehydrated in 50ml water)
50g grated carrot
finely grated zest of 1 orange
finely grated zest of 1½ lemons

Preheat the oven to 140°C/Gas 1. Grease a 20cm square or 23cm round cake tin with a little sunflower oil and line it with 3 layers of baking parchment.

Sift the flour into a large bowl, add the sultanas, raisins, dates, bicarb, salt, cardamom and mixed spice and stir well. Add the barley malt syrup and brown rice syrup and mix them in thoroughly. Stir in the beaten eggs, then the sunflower oil. Add the pineapple and the water you soaked it in, grated carrot and orange and lemon zest and give it all a good old stir until everything is well combined.

Spoon the mixture into the prepared baking tin – it should reach about three-quarters of the way up the tin. Cover the top with a sheet of greaseproof paper and put the cake in the preheated oven. Bake for 2 hours and 15 minutes, then test it with a skewer inserted into the centre of the cake. If the skewer comes out more or less clean, the cake is cooked. If not, put it back in the oven for another 15 minutes, then test again. The cake might need up to 2 hours and 45 minutes, depending on your oven and tin.

Once the cake is cooked, take it out of the oven and leave it to cool in the tin. Then transfer it to a wire rack and allow to cool completely. Wrap the cake in greaseproof paper and foil and store in a cool, dry place until Christmas. If you want to add marzipan and icing, have a look at page 72. But if, like us, you hate marzipan, glaze the cake with warm apricot jam and top with halved roasted almonds arranged in a decorative fashion.

And if you want to make your Christmas cake extra boozy, feed it once a week! Make some holes in the top with a skewer and carefully pour over some brandy, rum or calvados. Allow it to soak in, then wrap the cake up again.

CHRISTMAS PUDDING ICE CREAM

This is our special Christmas ice cream, studded with brandy-soaked fruit and crunchy nuts and capped with melted chocolate. When you're ready to eat, remove the ice cream from the freezer and leave it at room temperature for five minutes before serving.

SERVES 6

300ml double cream
300ml whole milk
5 large free-range egg yolks
75g golden caster sugar
finely grated zest and juice of 2 well-scrubbed oranges
50g raisins
50g sultanas
50g glacé cherries, quartered
50g dried no-soak apricots, cut into sixths
50g good-quality candied peel, diced
2 balls of stem ginger in syrup, drained and diced (optional)
4 tbsp cherry brandy
4 tbsp brandy
1 tsp ground mixed spice
60g almonds, cut into slivers

CHOCOLATE COATING
100g plain dark chocolate
25g butter

Pour the cream and milk into a large, non-stick pan, bring to the boil, then remove from the heat. Whisk the egg yolks with the sugar in a bowl until pale and add the warm milk and cream, whisking constantly. Stir in the zest and juice, then return the liquid to the pan. Place over a low heat and cook for 10 minutes, stirring constantly, until the custard coats the back of a wooden spoon. Don't overheat or the mixture will become grainy.

Remove the custard from the heat and pour it into a large bowl. Cover with clingfilm and leave to cool for at least an hour. Put the dried fruit, candied peel and stem ginger, if using, in a small pan and add the cherry brandy, brandy and mixed spice. Bring to a gentle simmer and cook for 2 minutes, stirring constantly. Tip into a bowl and leave to cool. Preheat the oven to 190°C/Gas 5. Scatter the almonds evenly onto a baking tray and bake in the centre of the oven for 8–10 minutes or until golden brown, turning once. Leave to cool. Line a 1.5 litre pudding basin with two layers of clingfilm, leaving plenty hanging over the edges.

When the custard has cooled completely, pour it into an ice cream maker and churn for 45–60 minutes or until the mixture is very thick. Transfer it to a large bowl and quickly stir in the dried fruit and all but 1 tablespoon of the toasted nuts. Spoon into the prepared basin, smooth the surface and cover with the overhanging clingfilm. Freeze for 1 hour, then remove from the freezer and gently stir with a spoon to mix any fruit that has sunk to the bottom into the ice cream again. Cover with the clingfilm and return to the freezer overnight and for up to a week before serving. Keep the reserved nuts in a jar.

Up to 2 hours before serving, melt the chocolate with the butter in a heatproof bowl over a pan of simmering water until smooth. Remove from the heat and leave to cool for 20 minutes. Take the ice cream out of the freezer and turn it out onto a freezer-proof plate. Peel off the clingfilm. Pour the chocolate sauce over the ice cream. Sprinkle with the reserved nuts and return it to the freezer at once. Leave to set for up to 3 hours before serving.

BLACKCURRANT & CASSIS SORBET

Sorbets are wonderfully refreshing little touches of sweetness – very welcome over the festive season – and surprisingly easy to make. Check out our special way of making sorbets if you don't have an ice cream maker. The recipe for the gin and tonic sorbet shown overleaf is on page 185.

SERVES 6

200g caster sugar
450g frozen blackcurrants or forest fruits
freshly squeezed juice of ½ lemon
2 tbsp cassis (blackcurrant liqueur)
sprigs of mint or fresh berries

First make the sugar syrup. Put 150g of the sugar and 300ml of water in a pan and slowly bring to the boil, stirring occasionally. Boil for 5 minutes, then remove from the heat and set aside.

Put the blackcurrants in a clean pan with the remaining 50g of sugar and the lemon juice. Cook over a low heat for 10 minutes or until the fruits are softened, stirring occasionally. Blitz with a stick blender or in a food processor, then press through a fine sieve into the sugar syrup. Add the cassis and stir well. Leave to cool. Pour the mixture into an ice cream maker and churn to a soft sorbet-like consistency. Tip into a freezer-proof container and freeze for at least 6 hours before serving. Scoop the sorbet into tumblers and decorate with sprigs of mint or fresh berries.

If you don't have an ice cream maker, pour the cooled fruit mixture into a freezer-proof container and freeze for about 2 hours until ice crystals have formed all around the edges. Remove and beat with an electric whisk or bash vigorously with a fork until smooth, then return to the freezer. Repeat the method twice more, returning to the freezer for about 2 hours each time, until the sorbet is smooth and fine-textured. Then freeze until solid.

EASIEST-EVER MANGO SORBET

SERVES 6

2 x 425g cans of mango slices in syrup

Tip the mango slices and syrup into a food processor and blend into a purée. Press through a fine sieve into a bowl to remove any tough fibres. Tip the pulp into an ice cream maker and churn until the mixture has a soft, sorbet-like consistency. This may take up to an hour. Transfer it to a freezer-proof container and freeze for at least 6 hours before serving.

When you're ready to serve, take the sorbet out of the freezer and leave at room temperature for 5 minutes. Scoop the sorbet out and serve in tumblers or pretty bowls.

What's your Christmas tipple?

Perhaps it's that funny liqueur you picked up on holiday or a classic from a bygone era, like a snowball or port and lemon. Or maybe you'll splash out on a swanky bottle of wine or two. And then there's beer. We spoke to beer writer **Jeff Pickthall** to find out more.

Beer is so omnipresent, so taken for granted that it's easy to overlook it as a drink for special occasions. But beyond the mass-market brands there is a thriving culture of beer appreciation. Connoisseurs sniff, swirl and sip flavour-packed beers in a glorious multiplicity of styles and, increasingly, beer lovers are realising that their favourite drink has a very big trick up its sleeve – it goes brilliantly with food. Wine fans will swear that their beverage is the only one to go with food – they're wrong. There are thousands of beers to choose from, including Christmas beers, so it is really worth looking for something special.

Beer with the bird

Hops in beer serve the dual role of providing bitterness and countering malt sweetness; they offer attractive fruit and herbal flavours and aromas of their own. As turkey isn't the most assertive of meats, a highly hopped beer is likely to overwhelm your bird, so golden or brown beers with moderate hopping are worth seeking out. Some styles to look out for are: dark lagers from the Czech Republic; German Oktoberfest or Märzen lagers; amber beers from the USA; Bière de Gardes from France; dubbels from Belgium. Also, every British craft brewery – there are more than six hundred now – produces one or more malty beers.

One of the key advantages of beer compared to wine is that its carbonation (fizziness) continually refreshes the palate. This phenomenon is particularly noticeable where fats are concerned; try it when sneaking a few chipolatas wrapped in bacon before the bird is served.

The end of the meal

Christmas pudding works with beer surprisingly well. By this stage of the day, you're probably wanting to slacken your belt so large volumes of beer may not appeal. Fortunately, the best beer match is strong and consumed in small quantities. The style is barley wine. Don't be misled, this beer style has nothing at all to do with grapes; the name refers to its high strength. Some barley wines do reach the 12% alcohol content typical of most wines and they tend to be rich, warming and sweetish with honey and caramel notes. Alternatively, recognising Christmas pudding's sumptuous dried fruit content, German doppelbocks and Belgian bruns partner well. In both cases, the specialist yeast strains create flavours that are commonly described with words such as 'raisiny', and even 'rum-like'.

Many families have a tradition of serving a big hunk of Stilton or other strong cheese at Christmas. For this, I think beer really is the only option – don't let anyone serve you wine with a big-flavour cheese, not even fortified wine. For assertive blue-veined cheeses you need stout. As if by magic, stout's roasted, toasted flavours go with cheese like no wine ever can. If you're brave you may like to try an 'imperial stout'. These are stouts on steroids.

"One of the advantages of beer compared to wine is that its carbonation (fizziness) continually refreshes the palate…"

Their intense tarry flavours work wonders with salty and acidic cheeses. Once again, beer's carbonation is a crucial advantage in keeping the palate fresh.

Don't forget the leftovers

An unavoidable, but delightful, feature of Christmas feasting is eating up leftovers. At one time or another, we've all rustled up a turkey curry. By definition, a curry has lots of spicy flavours and most people will opt for a bland, freezing-cold lager to drink with it. That's all very well for taking the edge off chilli heat, but extra flavour pleasures are sacrificed. The beer style for spicy food is IPA – India Pale Ale. There are no spices in IPAs but they are heavily hopped and hops add a big variety of flavours and aromas. IPAs are often described as 'piny', 'citrusy', 'fruity', 'herby', and 'fragrant'. They also tend to be dry with only minimal

sweetness. Their flavours are big enough not to be eclipsed by spices. In recent years, American craft brewers have latched on to IPAs and upped the flavours to the max. Only spicy food can keep up!

If wine is your tipple

You might want to treat yourself to something a bit special for Christmas so here are some of our favourites. For celebrations or before the big meal, we like something sparkling – good prosecco and cava are cheaper than champagne and can be even tastier. Or how about starting the meal with our gin and tonic sorbet (see page 185). Flavoursome whites include white burgundy, such as Meursault, or Gavi de Gavi – an Italian wine. For reds, try Fleurie, Beaune, Barolo or Si's favourite Sicilian red, La Planeta. The pud can be a challenge, but ice wine, muscat and vin santo are all good choices.

Edible
gifts

LAST-MINUTE CHRISTMAS CHUTNEY

This is a brilliant, fruity accompaniment to cold meats and just the thing to liven up cold cuts or a buffet table. We've found it works really well with cheese too, so we like to serve some on the cheeseboard at the end of a meal. And, you're more than likely to have lots of the ingredients in stock if you've been doing a bit of Christmas baking. If you don't have any of the dried fruit that we've suggested, simply swap them for something you do have. Sultanas and dried pears work well in place of the raisins and figs, for instance. This can even be made on the day it is going to be served, as it doesn't need maturing like traditional chutney.

MAKES ABOUT 3 JARS

1 tbsp sunflower oil
2 medium red onions, halved and sliced
2 garlic cloves, finely chopped
2 tsp finely chopped fresh root ginger or stem ginger in syrup, drained and finely chopped
200g dried no-soak apricots, quartered
150g soft dried figs, quartered
100g raisins
150g demerara sugar
150g white wine vinegar
¼ whole nutmeg, finely grated
1 cinnamon stick
1 tsp sea salt flakes
freshly ground black pepper

Heat the oil in a large non-stick saucepan and fry the onions over a low heat for about 10 minutes until very soft. Add the garlic and ginger and cook for 2–3 minutes more, then increase the heat slightly and fry for a further 4–5 minutes until the onions begin to brown, stirring constantly.

Tip the apricots, figs and raisins into the pan and cook with the onions for 2–3 minutes until the fruit begins to swell. Sprinkle over the sugar, add the vinegar, spices, salt and plenty of freshly ground black pepper. Stir well, bring to a gentle simmer over a low to medium heat and cook, uncovered, for 30 minutes. Stir occasionally, especially towards the end of the cooking time when the chutney is more likely to stick.

The chutney is ready when the liquid has reduced to just 4–5 tablespoons and the fruit looks plump and glossy. Remove the pan from the heat and leave the chutney to cool. The fruit will continue absorbing the liquid as it cools, so you just need to give it a quick stir before putting it into serving dishes or carefully sterilised jars. Use greaseproof circles to cover the tops if the jars have metal lids or the vinegar will rot the lids.

If you're giving the chutney as presents, top the jars with pretty fabric covers and tie with ribbons. This chutney needs to be kept in the fridge and used within a month so it's a good idea to add that info to your labels.

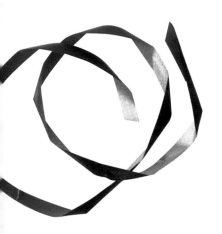

CHRISTMAS PUDDING VODKA

Keep this delicious drink in the freezer for a refreshing – and surprising – Christmas treat. Make bottles for gifts too, but don't forget to warn people that the contents are almost pure vodka. You don't want auntie falling face first into the turkey! Use a reasonably good vodka, not the discount stuff.

MAKES 1 x 500ML BOTTLE

300g mixed dried fruit
75g caster sugar
2 cinnamon sticks
2 tsp ground mixed spice
6 cloves
½ whole nutmeg, finely grated
finely grated zest of 1 well-scrubbed orange
finely grated zest of 1 unwaxed lemon
75cl bottle of decent vodka

Mix the dried fruit with the sugar, cinnamon sticks, mixed spice, cloves, grated nutmeg and zest in a large bowl. Pour over the vodka and cover tightly with clingfilm. Place in the fridge and leave for 3 days, stirring once a day.

Line a sieve with double layer of fine muslin and place it over a large, clean jug. Pour the dried fruit and vodka mixture into the sieve and leave it to drip through into the jug. Pour into a clean, dry bottle and fasten the lid. Store in the freezer until needed.

SLOE GIN

Sloe, sloe, prick, prick, sloe – making sloe gin is one of those jobs that shows that Christmas really is on its way. First you have to find your sloes. They're the fruit of the blackthorn bush, which often grows in hedgerows, so ask around and make sure you know exactly what you're picking. The best time to pick sloes is in October after the first frost, but don't leave it too late or your sloe gin won't be ready for Christmas. Some people simulate the first frost by putting the berries in the freezer overnight before making the gin.

MAKES 1 LITRE

500g sloes
1 litre gin
250g caster sugar
lots of patience

Each sloe has to be popped with a knife or pricked with a needle, so settle down for an hour or two and start stabbing.

Place the pricked sloes in a demijohn or other container. Pour over the gin, add the sugar and shake well. Shake the mixture twice a week for the first 4 weeks, then once a week after that. It should be nicely matured by Christmas. Strain off the liqueur into nice bottles and discard the berries. Lovely!

CHOCOLATE ORANGE-CRISP TRUFFLES

Rich, dark and creamy, these truffles contain deliciously crisp pieces of orange caramel
and make a fab after-dinner treat with coffee. They also make gorgeous gifts for friends and family.

MAKES ABOUT 36

200g plain dark chocolate,
broken into squares
150ml double cream
25g unsalted butter
2 tbsp orange-flavoured liqueur, such as
Cointreau or Grand Marnier
1–2 tsp orange flower water (optional)

ORANGE CRACKNEL
150g caster sugar
1 medium orange

DECORATION
50–75g good quality white chocolate,
chilled, then grated

Don't take the syrup off the heat too soon or it will be chewy rather than crisp. Watch it very carefully as once it has changed to a golden caramel colour it will burn in an instant.

Put the chocolate into a non-stick pan with the cream, butter and liqueur. Heat very gently, stirring constantly, until you have a rich, smooth sauce, but don't let it overheat. Stir in the orange flower water to taste. Mix well over a low heat, stirring with a wooden spoon, then pour the sauce into a heatproof bowl and leave to cool. Cover with clingfilm and chill in the fridge for about 1½ hours until firm.

To make the orange cracknel, line a small baking sheet with baking parchment. Put the sugar in a small non-stick pan. Peel half the orange in wide strips, using a potato peeler. You want the zest only, so make sure you don't peel off any pith with it. Put the zest strips in the pan with the sugar.

Cut the orange in half and squeeze out the juice. Add enough water to top the juice up to 100ml if necessary. Pour the juice over the sugar in the pan and place over a low heat until the sugar dissolves, stirring regularly. Increase the heat and boil the syrup for 5 minutes. Remove the zest carefully using tongs and discard. Continue boiling the syrup for at least 10 minutes until it starts to deepen in colour. Drop a little onto a cold plate and it should harden at once. Pour the hot syrup onto the prepared tray very carefully and leave to cool for at least 30 minutes.

Remove the chocolate mixture from the fridge. Turn the hardened syrup out onto a work surface lined with another sheet of baking parchment and bash it into small shards. Stir the pieces into the chocolate, then chill the mixture for 1 hour.

Scatter some of the grated white chocolate onto a plate. Using a teaspoon, scoop spoonfuls of the chocolate mixture out of the bowl and roll into small balls in your hands. Drop each ball onto the white chocolate as soon as it is formed and roll it around until evenly covered. The warmth of your hands will begin to melt the truffle mixture and will help the white chocolate to stick. Top up the white chocolate as needed. Chill before serving. Gobble the truffles up yourself or put them in pretty bags to give as presents. They keep in the fridge for a few days.

CREAMY CHRISTMAS FUDGE

This dreamy, creamy fudge has just a hint of spice, ginger and plump dried fruit. Using a sugar thermometer makes it much easier to cook the fudge to the right point so it's well worth getting one.

MAKES 36 PIECES

150g butter, cubed, plus extra for greasing
50g mixed dried fruit
3 balls of stem ginger in syrup, drained
and cut into small pieces
100ml dark spiced rum,
such as Captain Morgan
1 cinnamon stick
2 star anise
1 x 397g can of evaporated milk
500g granulated sugar

Grease an 18cm square cake tin or a 26 x 16cm rectangular tin and line the base and sides with baking parchment. Grease the parchment and set aside. Put the dried fruit, ginger and rum in a small non-stick pan with the cinnamon and star anise. Bring the rum to the boil and cook until it has completely evaporated or been absorbed by the fruit, stirring constantly. Remove from the heat and leave to cool.

Put the 150g butter, evaporated milk and sugar in a non-stick pan and cook over a low heat until the sugar dissolves, stirring regularly. Increase the heat and bring the mixture to the boil. It will boil furiously to begin with, so make sure your saucepan is large enough to hold the mixture without it boiling over.

Cook for 20–30 minutes, stirring constantly and carefully with a wooden spoon to stop the fudge catching and burning on the bottom of the pan. Watch out – it will be fiendishly hot. Put a sugar thermometer in the pan after about 20 minutes. You need the mixture to reach the soft ball stage, at 116°C, before taking it off the heat. If you don't have a thermometer, drop a little fudge into a bowl of ice-cold water. The fudge should immediately form a soft ball. Just before the fudge is ready, it will bubble less fiercely and look more like molten lava, so keep stirring as this is when it's most likely to stick.

When the fudge has reached the right point, remove it from the heat and stir energetically for 3 minutes before adding the spiced fruit and ginger – take out the cinnamon and star anise. Continue stirring for another 6–8 minutes as the fudge thickens. As the fudge cools, it will gradually change from a thick, creamy mixture to form a ball in the centre of the saucepan. Keep stirring and when the fudge begins to look grainy and loses its glossy appearance, put it into the tin. It will be very stiff at this stage, so you'll need to press it into all the corners. Smooth the surface and set the fudge aside to cool completely. After 3–4 hours you should be able to cut it into small squares or little rectangles ready for serving. Store in an airtight container or put the fudge into little gift bags. Eat within a week or so.

If the fudge does burn and small brown flecks suddenly appear, remove the pan from the heat and put the base in a sink of cold water to stop the fudge cooking. Then tip the fudge into a clean pan without further stirring and you should be able to rescue the rest of the mixture.

CHOCOLATE ORANGE & CRANBERRY BISCOTTI

These make good-sized biscotti, just right to serve with freshly poured coffee. For more delicate titbits, divide the dough into three portions instead of two. The orange-flavoured chocolate tastes amazing, but you can use a plain chocolate instead and add finely grated orange zest in place of the vanilla extract if you prefer.

MAKES ABOUT 60

375g plain flour, plus extra for dusting
1½ tsp baking powder
200g caster sugar
100g good quality orange-flavoured chocolate (such as Green & Black's Maya Gold)
75g blanched almonds
100g dried cranberries
3 large free-range eggs
1 tsp vanilla extract

Preheat the oven to 180°C/Gas 4. Put the flour in a large bowl and stir in the baking powder and sugar. Chop the chocolate into small pieces and put them in a colander. Shake them about a bit to get rid of any tiny pieces of chocolate, then tip the rest into the bowl with the flour.

Stir in the almonds and cranberries. Beat the eggs with the vanilla extract and pour them onto the flour mixture. Mix with a wooden spoon and then with your hands until the ingredients come together and form a stiff but pliable dough.

Transfer the dough to a well-floured board and divide it into 2 equal pieces. Roll each one into a fat sausage-shape of about 25cm long. Put the rolls of dough on a large baking tray, lined with baking parchment, leaving plenty of room between each one to allow for spreading. Flatten them slightly so they are about 2cm high.

Bake for 25–30 minutes until the dough is risen and firm but still looks fairly pale. Leave to cool on the baking sheet for 10 minutes. Reduce the oven temperature to 140°C/Gas 1. Transfer the dough to a board and, using a bread knife, cut into slices about 1cm thick.

Return the biscuits to the baking tray and bake for another 20 minutes or until very lightly browned. The biscotti will become crisp as they dry. Leave to cool, then store in an airtight container for up to 2 weeks. They also make great Christmas gifts.

CANDIED PEEL

This can be used in cakes and bakes, enjoyed just as it is, or dipped in chocolate as a home-made treat with coffee at the end of a meal. Also makes great festive gifts.

MAKES ENOUGH FOR A 750ML JAR OR 6 SMALL CELLOPHANE BAGS

1 large grapefruit
2 large oranges
1 large unwaxed lemon
500g caster sugar

CHOCOLATE-COVERED PEEL
100g plain dark chocolate (minimum 70% cocoa solids), broken into squares

Wash all the fruit in warm water and scrub well to help remove any wax or other chemicals from the skin. Cut the ends off each fruit, then remove the peel with a sharp knife, keeping as much pith attached as possible. Scrape out any fruit flesh that gets caught.

Cut the peel into long strips, 5–7mm wide. Put all the peel in a large saucepan and cover with cold water. Bring to the boil, then drain the peel in a colander and return to the pan. Cover again with fresh cold water and bring to the boil. Reduce the heat to a simmer, cover the saucepan loosely with a lid and cook for 30 minutes. Drain the peel in a colander.

Put the sugar in a medium saucepan with 250ml of cold water. Stir over a low heat until the sugar dissolves, then bring to the boil and immediately remove from the heat. Stir the peel into the sugar syrup and return the pan to the heat. Bring to the boil, then reduce the heat and simmer very gently for about an hour or until almost all the liquid has evaporated and the peel is covered in a thick, glossy syrup. Stir occasionally as the syrup reduces. If the syrup begins to crystallise, add a little water and warm through gently.

Line a large tray or cooling rack with baking parchment. Using tongs or a couple of forks, arrange the candied peel in rows, spacing them evenly apart on the paper. Leave in a warm, dry place overnight to harden. If the peel still feels a little damp the next day, leave for a few more hours.

When the candied peel is dry, chop it into small pieces to use in baking, eat it just as it is, or cover it with chocolate. Store the peel in an airtight jar. For presents, divide the peel into cellophane bags and tie tightly with colourful ribbon. Stored in a cool, dark place, the candied peel will last for several months and the chocolate-covered peel for at least two weeks.

To make the chocolate coating, melt the chocolate in a heatproof bowl over a pan of gently simmering water. Dip one end of each strip of peel into the chocolate, then twirl around a couple of times until evenly covered and no longer dripping. Place immediately on a baking tray lined with baking parchment and leave to set for at least an hour.

PANETTONE

A simple version of the fantastic Italian-style loaf that's often eaten at Christmas.
Use any leftovers to make an extra-special bread and butter pudding.

MAKES 1 LARGE LOAF

300ml semi skimmed milk
3 tsp vanilla extract
115g butter, cut into small pieces, plus extra
for greasing
75g soft light brown sugar
600g strong plain flour, plus extra for dusting
½ tsp sea salt
7g sachet of fast-action dried yeast
finely grated zest of 1 well-scrubbed orange
finely grated zest of 1 unwaxed lemon
1 medium free-range egg, beaten
sunflower oil, for greasing
150g mixed dried fruit
icing sugar, to decorate

Pour the milk into a saucepan and add the vanilla, 100g of the butter and the sugar. Place over a medium heat until the butter is melted and the mixture is lukewarm. Don't allow it to get too hot. Remove the pan from the heat and set aside.

Put the flour in a large bowl and stir in the salt, yeast and zest. Stir the beaten egg into the warm milk and pour onto the flour mixture. Mix with a wooden spoon and then with your hands until the mixture forms a soft, spongy dough. Turn it out onto a well-floured surface and knead for 10 minutes. The dough will be fairly wet to begin with, but within a few minutes it should feel less sticky.

Put the dough in a greased bowl, cover with lightly oiled clingfilm and leave to rise in a warm place for 1 hour or until doubled in size and very puffy. Grease a 16–18cm cake tin and line with a deep double layer of baking parchment, making sure it overlaps and stands well above the top of the tin to allow the dough to rise. Line the base of the tin with a circle of baking parchment.

Transfer the dough to a floured surface and punch it back down, then shape it into a 20cm round. Scatter half the dried fruit over the dough and knead it in for a minute or two. Scatter over the remaining fruit and knead into the dough thoroughly. Roll the dough into a large ball and place it in the prepared tin. Leave to rise for a further 45–60 minutes or until doubled in size.

Preheat the oven to 200°C/Gas 6. Melt the remaining butter in a small pan. Cut a deep cross in the surface of the dough and remove any loose bits of dried fruit from the surface, so they don't burn. Brush the butter over the surface of the dough and into the cuts. Bake in the centre of the oven for 35–45 minutes until well risen and deep golden brown.

Remove the panettone from the oven and leave to cool in the tin for 15 minutes. Then take it out of the tin, strip off the baking parchment and cool on a wire rack. Sprinkle with sifted icing sugar before serving if you like. Store in a large plastic bag.

PANFORTE

This dense Italian cake contains lots of spice, dried fruit and nuts so it's ideal for Christmas. It keeps well too, so it's good for presents. There's a picture of it with the panettone on the previous page.

MAKES 12–16 SLICES

sunflower oil, for greasing
125g whole blanched almonds
125g whole blanched hazelnuts
200g runny honey
150g caster sugar
125g mixed candied peel, chopped
100g dried figs, chopped
finely grated zest of 1 well-scrubbed orange
2 tbsp cocoa powder
1 tsp ground mixed spice
½ tsp ground cinnamon
½ tsp ground allspice
edible rice paper or icing sugar, to decorate

Preheat the oven to 200°C/Gas 6. Grease a 20cm loose-based flan tin and line it with baking parchment. Brush with sunflower oil and set aside.

Tip the nuts onto a large baking tray and bake in the centre of the preheated oven for 8–10 minutes, turning once or twice until they are pale golden brown all over. Watch them carefully as they can burn very easily while your back's turned. As soon as the nuts are ready, take them out of the oven and leave to cool for a few minutes.

Reduce the oven temperature to 150°C/Gas 2. Put the honey and sugar in a medium pan and cook over a low heat, stirring constantly until the sugar dissolves. Increase the heat and bring to the boil. Cook for 3–4 minutes or until the mixture reaches the 'soft ball' stage. This means that a little of the mixture should form a soft ball when dropped into a cup of cold water. Take great care not to overcook or the mixture will turn into toffee.

Remove the pan from the heat and quickly stir in the nuts, candied peel, dried fruit, zest, cocoa and spices. The mixture will stiffen quickly, so it is important to tip the whole lot into the prepared tin as soon as it is mixed. Smooth the surface with the back of a spoon, pressing down firmly. Tap the tin on the work surface to help level the surface.

Place on a baking tray and bake for 30–35 minutes or until the panforte rises slightly in the tin. Remove from the oven, leave to stand for 10 minutes and turn out onto a large sheet of rice paper or baking parchment. Place another sheet of rice paper on top and leave to cool. When the cake is completely cold, you can trim the rice paper so it fits neatly over the cake.

If you can't get hold of rice paper, cool the cake and then dust with sifted icing sugar. Cut into narrow wedges to serve.

Festive
feasts

CHESTNUT, ROASTED BUTTERNUT SQUASH & BRAMLEY APPLE SOUP

This is a great winter soup, packed with festive flavours and perfect with our cheese straws (see page 168). The Bramley apple is the secret, as it tempers the sweetness of the chestnuts and squash.

SERVES 10

1.5kg butternut squash,
cut into large chunks
5 tbsp olive oil,
plus extra for cooking the squash
1 onion, chopped
1 garlic clove, crushed
2 potatoes, diced
1 Bramley apple, cored and chopped
2 litres chicken or vegetable stock
1 sprig of thyme
2 bay leaves
400g chestnut purée
500g chestnuts, peeled and roasted
(set aside a handful for garnish)
sea salt flakes
freshly ground black pepper
cream for garnish (optional)
truffle oil for garnish (optional)

Preheat the oven to 200°C/Gas 6. Put the chunks of squash in a roasting tin and splash with 3 tablespoons of the olive oil. Give them a stir so they are all coated with oil. Roast the squash in the hot oven for 30 minutes or until they are cooked through and a bit scorched, then set aside to cool. When the squash is cool enough, drain off the oil and remove the peel from the chunks.

Heat the remaining 2 tablespoons of olive oil in a big soup pan, add the onion, garlic, potatoes and apple and fry until softened, not browned. Add the stock, squash, thyme, bay leaves, chestnut purée and chestnuts – don't forget to keep some chestnuts back for the garnish. Season to taste.

Simmer until the potatoes are soft, stirring regularly so the soup doesn't catch and burn on the bottom of the pan. Leave to cool slightly, then purée in a blender. Pour the soup back into the pan, check the seasoning and warm through.

Ladle into bowls and garnish with a swirl of cream and another of truffle oil if you like. Top with slices of the reserved chestnuts.

FESTIVE DUCK BREASTS
WITH LEMON & THYME POLENTA

This dish is ideal for a Christmas treat when you've packed the kids off to bed and there's just the two of you. Quick and easy to prepare and truly delicious.

SERVES 2

2 duck breasts, skin on
2 star anise
1 cinnamon stick
2 cloves
finely grated zest of ½ orange
150ml Marsala wine
100ml chicken stock
good-quality cranberry sauce
1 sprig of thyme
a pinch of lemon zest
sea salt flakes
freshly ground black pepper

POLENTA
125g polenta
50g unsalted butter
1 tsp chopped fresh thyme
finely grated zest of 1 lemon
sea salt flakes
freshly ground black pepper

Rub the skin of the duck breasts with sea salt flakes and freshly ground pepper and place them skin side down in a dry, preheated frying pan.

Cook the duck for 6 minutes on each side over a medium heat if you like it pink or 8 minutes on each side if you prefer it murdered.

While the duck is cooking, you can get on with preparing the polenta. Bring 575ml of water to the boil in a saucepan and add the polenta in a steady stream, whisking all the time until it thickens – about 3–4 minutes should do it. Remove the pan from the heat. Add the butter, thyme and lemon zest and mix well, then season to taste. Leave for a few minutes to let those lovely flavours infuse the polenta.

Now back to the duck. Remove the duck from the frying pan and set it aside to rest. Add the star anise, cinnamon, cloves and orange zest to the pan you cooked the duck in, then pour in the Marsala wine and chicken stock and deglaze those lovely duck juices. Reduce the liquid over a high heat for 3 minutes or so to intensify the flavours and thicken the sauce, then have a taste and season.

Carve the duck breast on the diagonal and place the slices on top of the polenta. Pour over the reduced sauce and add a teaspoon of cranberry sauce on top of the duck. Garnish with a sprig of thyme and a pinch of lemon zest.

Serve with whatever you fancy, but we like this with green beans.

SPICED BEEF
WITH ROOT VEGETABLES

This hearty beef dish is perfect for a cold winter's night. It's dead easy to chuck together and can be left gently simmering away until meltingly tender. The spices give it a wonderful warmth and the addition of assorted vegetables adds colour and saves on the washing up – it's a one-pot dish. Serve with creamy mashed potatoes or bung in a few new potatoes and braise them with the other vegetables for an hour. If you have any beef leftover, it's delicious sliced and served cold with lots of horseradish sauce.

SERVES 6–8

2kg rolled beef brisket
3 tbsp sunflower oil
500ml red wine
2 tbsp tomato purée
1 tbsp dark brown soft sugar
500ml hot beef stock, fresh or made with a cube
1 cinnamon stick
3 bay leaves
8 cloves
1 tsp yellow mustard seeds
16 small shallots, peeled
3 large carrots, peeled and cut into short lengths
4 medium parsnips, peeled and quartered lengthways
4 turnips, peeled and quartered
4 garlic cloves, peeled and halved
2 tbsp cornflour, blended with 2 tbsp cold water

SPICE MIX
1 tbsp whole allspice
1 tbsp coriander seeds
1 tsp cumin seeds
2 tsp sea salt flakes
1 tsp coarsely ground black pepper

First prepare the spice mixture. Grind the allspice, coriander, cumin, sea salt and black pepper together in a pestle and mortar until the mixture is powdery.

Preheat the oven to 180°C/Gas 4. Place the beef on a board and pat it dry with kitchen paper. Rub the beef all over with 1 tablespoon of the oil. Scatter the spice powder on the board and roll the beef in it until it's evenly covered.

Heat the remaining oil in a large non-stick frying pan and fry the beef over a medium heat for 8–10 minutes, turning it every now and then until well browned on all sides. Transfer the beef to a large flame-proof casserole dish. Pour half the wine into the frying pan and bring to the boil, stirring constantly to lift the sediment from the bottom of the pan. Add the tomato purée and sugar and stir until dissolved.

Tip the wine mixture over the beef and add the rest of the wine, the stock, cinnamon stick, bay leaves, cloves and mustard seeds to the casserole dish. Bring to the boil, then cover with a lid and transfer to the oven. Cook for 2¼ hours.

Remove the casserole from the oven and turn the beef over. Place the shallots, carrots, parsnips, turnips and garlic around the beef. Cover with a lid and return to the oven for another hour. By this time the beef will be deliciously tender and the vegetables softened but still holding their shape.

Place the beef onto a warmed serving dish. Remove the vegetables with a slotted spoon and put them around the beef. Place the casserole dish over a medium heat and stir in the cornflour mixture. Cook for 1–2 minutes, stirring constantly, until the sauce has thickened. Strain the sauce into a warm jug and serve with the beef and vegetables.

If you don't have a suitable casserole dish in which to cook the beef, put it in a sturdy roasting tin and cover tightly with foil instead.

TRADITIONAL HONEY-GLAZED GAMMON

Cook a big piece of gammon to serve a party of 20 people or a smaller joint for a family meal – with lots of delicious leftovers. It tastes amazing served hot with a dribble of the cooking liquor, a generous spoonful of Cumberland sauce or a really delicious parsley sauce. Make sure you buy good-quality gammon. Double-smoked works a treat for this recipe if you can get your hands on some.

SERVES 10–20

2–4kg boned and rolled smoked gammon
2 small onions, peeled and halved
2 medium carrots, scrubbed and cut into short lengths
2 celery sticks, cut into short lengths
4 bay leaves
12 black peppercorns
small handful of whole cloves

GLAZE
4 tbsp runny honey
4 tbsp prepared English mustard

Put the gammon in a large saucepan and cover with cold water. Bring to the boil over a high heat, then remove the pan from the heat and drain all the water away. Refill the pan with fresh water, add the onions, carrots, celery, bay leaves and peppercorns. Return to the heat and bring to the boil. Reduce the heat, cover and leave the gammon to simmer gently for 20 minutes per 500g. If your pan isn't quite big enough for the water to cover the joint completely, turn it over halfway through the cooking time. When the gammon is ready, remove the pan from the heat and carefully lift the meat from the water and place it on a board. Leave to cool for 15 minutes. Don't throw the stock away – use it for making a delicious pea and ham soup.

Preheat the oven to 200°C/Gas 6. Using a small knife, carefully cut away and peel off the rind, leaving as much of the fat as possible. Score the fat in a diamond pattern and push a clove into the centre of each diamond. Line a roasting tin with a large piece of foil and place the gammon inside. Bring the sides of the foil up to create a bowl shape in which the gammon can nestle.

To make the glaze, mix the honey and mustard together until smooth and brush half evenly over the gammon, including the face. Bake in the centre of the oven for 10 minutes. Take out of the oven and brush the remaining honey mixture over the gammon. Put the meat back in the oven, placing the tin so the opposite side of the gammon is facing the back. Cook for 10–15 minutes until the fat is glossy and golden brown. If the top starts to get too brown in places, cover loosely with small pieces of foil. Leave to stand for about 15 minutes before carving.

Put the gammon on a serving platter or board. Pour any of the marinade that's collected in the foil into a small pan and warm it through gently. Carve the gammon into thin slices and serve dribbled with a little of the hot basting liquor to serve.

If serving the gammon cold, take it out of the fridge and leave it at room temperature for 30 minutes before eating.

LOIN OF VENISON
IN A SLOE GIN & BLACKBERRY GLAZE
WITH CANDIED SHALLOTS

This dish, cooked with the finest, most tender cut of venison, is a real treat. Use some of your home-made sloe gin (see page 30) to make the sweet, sticky glaze, which goes perfectly with the unctuous gooiness of the candied shallots. The shallots are also good with our spiced beef recipe (see page 49).

SERVES 6–8

1 saddle of venison, separated into 2 loins
1 tbsp olive oil
1 tsp dried thyme.
250g pancetta, thinly sliced
1 tbsp vegetable oil
2 tbsp sloe gin
200ml reduced beef stock
6 juniper berries, crushed
200g blackberries
knob of butter
sea salt flakes
freshly ground black pepper

CANDIED SHALLOTS
12 shallots, peeled
4 tbsp butter
1 tbsp caster sugar
75ml red wine
50ml port
50ml cassis
250ml good beef stock
1 bay leaf
½ tsp dried thyme
zest of ½ lemon

First trim the loins of any fat or sinew and wipe them clean. Rub the loins with olive oil, season lightly and rub in the dried thyme. Set aside. Preheat the oven to 180°C/Gas 4.

Lay the pancetta on a piece of clingfilm to make a pancetta sheet. Place the loin on one end of this and roll up so the loin is wrapped in pancetta, which will add flavour and keep the venison juicy. Remove the clingfilm. Warm the oil in a frying pan, the sort you can put into the oven. When the oil is hot, sear the loin until the pancetta is turning golden and the meat is sealed. Place the pan in the oven for 6–8 minutes. Don't leave it too long – the venison should still be pink. Remove the meat from the pan and set it somewhere warm to rest.

Deglaze the pan with sloe gin and burn off the alcohol. Pour in the beef stock and add the juniper berries. Simmer for about 5 minutes to reduce the stock further and infuse it with the juniper. Strain the sauce and return it to the pan, then add the blackberries. Cook for about 4 minutes until the blackberries are softened, then crush them slightly. Adjust the seasoning and whisk in the butter to give the sauce a velvety sheen. Discard the ends of the loin and cut the rest into thick slices. Allow about 3 slices per person and dress with the sloe and blackberry glaze. Serve with candied shallots and other veg of your choice.

CANDIED SHALLOTS
Bring a pan of water to the boil, add the shallots and simmer for 5 minutes to soften them up a bit. Melt the butter in a frying pan, add the shallots and cook them until brown. Add the sugar and stir until the butter starts to caramelise. Mix the wine, port, cassis and stock. Add about a quarter of this mixture to the shallots, bring to the boil and add the bay leaf, thyme and lemon zest. Keep adding the remaining liquid until the shallots are just covered with a glaze. Set aside until needed.

CHRISTMAS PUDDING FONDANTS

This is a great pudding for when you have people round for supper, as all the work can be done in advance and the puds are popped in the oven just before you are ready to eat them.

SERVES 6

50g mixed dried fruit
1 tsp mixed spice
2 tsp ground cinnamon
2 tsp ground nutmeg
finely grated zest of ½ orange
4 tbsp brandy
150g plain dark chocolate (70% cocoa solids)
150g butter, plus extra for greasing
3 large free-range eggs
3 large free-range egg yolks
50g caster sugar
25g self-raising flour
icing sugar

Grease 6 x 175ml metal pudding basins and line the bases with small discs of baking parchment. Place them on a small, sturdy baking tray. Put the dried fruit in a small pan with the spices, orange zest and brandy. Bring to the boil and simmer, stirring constantly, until the liquid evaporates or is absorbed by the fruit. Remove the pan from the heat and leave the fruit to cool for 30 minutes.

Break the chocolate into pieces and put them in a heatproof basin with the butter. Place the bowl over a pan of gently simmering water until the chocolate and butter have melted, stirring occasionally. Remove from the heat and leave to cool for 10 minutes.

Whisk the eggs, egg yolks and sugar together with an electric beater until pale and thick. Gently fold in the cooled fruit and the melted chocolate and butter. Sift the flour over the mixture and fold it in lightly. Spoon the mixture into the prepared basins and place them in the fridge for at least 30 minutes and up to 8 hours before cooking.

Preheat the oven to 200°C/Gas 6. About fifteen minutes before you want to serve the puddings, remove them from the fridge and bake for 10–11 minutes, until well risen but still wobbly in the middle. Add a minute to the cooking time for each hour that the puddings have chilled – up to 3 minutes extra.

Loosen the sides of the puddings with a round-bladed knife, turn them out onto dessert plates and remove the baking parchment. Dust the puddings with icing sugar and serve with crème fraîche, cream or brandy butter.

Turkey –
not just for Christmas

Christmas and turkeys go together. Get a good, traditional Bronze turkey, cook it right and you'll have a feast on the day, with plenty of leftovers for scrumptious sandwiches, turkey soup and other dishes.

The Bronze used to be the main turkey available in this country before supermarkets started selling the white breed, but its dark feather stubs were deemed to be ugly, and the Bronze all but disappeared. The white turkeys were fast growing so reached a large size at a young age and could be sold cheap, but they had little flavour. For years, the white gave turkey a bad name. People shoved a big bird in the oven for hours and served up dry, bland meat. Now, with the reappearance of the traditional Bronze bird – free-range, properly reared and dry plucked – you can cook your turkey for a shorter time with delicious results. Turkey is once again a great choice for the meal of the year.

A traditional, farm-produced Bronze, so called for the colour of its plumage, is about six months old when sold for Christmas. The average white turkey is only 12–13 weeks and a supermarket bronze is 13–18 weeks. Ask if the bird you're thinking of buying has been dry plucked and hung. If the answer is yes, it will be mature. The longer lifespan is all-important, as exercise and maturity gives flavourful meat – the sign of a mature bird is dark leg meat. Also, a mature turkey has fat marbling through the meat, which brings flavour and allows the meat to cook more quickly, just like a well-marbled steak.

We talked turkey with Paul Kelly, an Essex farmer who produces the award-winning KellyBronze birds (see page 224), and he is adamant that a turkey is much more than a Christmas dinner. He likens a big turkey to a lamb as an animal of many parts to be cooked in different ways and eaten throughout the year. Many people nowadays like to buy a turkey crown, the whole breast section, as a slightly smaller roast, but he urges his customers to buy the whole bird – it costs very little more than the crown. You can then use the back end (with all the dark meat) to make different meals. Or, have the whole turkey jointed and use it to make a range of dishes. And because the birds are raised traditionally to very high standards, they don't need to be cooked to destruction – the meat can even be eaten pink (take care, though as this doesn't apply to regular supermarket turkeys). Here's what Paul suggests:

Crown

The crown is made up of both breasts on the bone so you have all the delicious white meat. The wings are usually attached. You can remove them but they help keep the joint steady in the tin as it roasts. Cook in the same way as a whole turkey, according to weight, and serve with all the trimmings.

Back end

This is all the dark meat of the bird and can be roasted as one piece or jointed. Ask your butcher to remove the back end or do it yourself if you're handy with a carving knife. To remove the back end, make a deep cut between breast and leg, cutting through the skin right down to the back of the bird. Repeat on the other side so that all the skin attaching the legs to the bird is cut through. Then take the bird in your hands and break the back end away from the crown.

Legs

The leg of a big turkey makes a great roast, like a leg of lamb, and can be cooked pink if that's the way you like it. Remember that this applies to properly reared Bronze turkeys only. The leg can also be jointed into thigh and drumstick.

Thighs

Bone and trim the thigh, flatten it out slightly and cook it like a steak. Thigh meat makes great kebabs and curries too. You can also make mince from the thigh and leg meat. Turkey mince has half the saturated fat of beef.

Drumsticks

These can be roasted or they are great in a casserole, like coq au vin. Can also be boiled, marinated, then barbecued.

Breast

A whole breast can be removed from the bone and roasted. Or the breast can be cut across into steaks of about 5mm thick and pan-fried like escalopes, or used for stir fries. The inner fillet of the breast can be removed and cooked separately – it is wonderfully tender, rather like pork loin.

Wings

Like drumsticks, these can be boiled, marinated, then barbecued.

Carcass

Don't waste this. The carcass makes the best stock (see page 108) and soup (see page 129).

Christmas
baking

BANGING BANANA, WALNUT & SULTANA BREAD

This is a recipe we've had for years and it's a great way of using up black bananas. In fact, we find that the more repulsive looking the bananas, the better the bread. Makes good muffins, too.

MAKES 1 LOAF

225g self-raising flour
½ tsp salt
125g butter
150g caster sugar
2 free-range eggs, lightly beaten
170g shelled walnuts, broken into pieces
170g sultanas
450g bananas, the ripest ones you can find

Preheat the oven to 180°C/Gas 4. Grease a 900g loaf tin and sprinkle the inside with flour.

Tip the flour into a large mixing bowl, add the salt and mix together. Cut the butter into cubes and rub it into the flour with your fingers until the mixture has a crumb-like texture. Add the caster sugar and the eggs and mix thoroughly, then stir in the walnuts and sultanas. Mash the bananas in a separate bowl and when they are really sludgified, fold them into the mixture.

Spoon the mixture into the prepared loaf tin and bake for about an hour. Ovens vary, of course, so keep an eye on your banana bread – if it looks black and crunchy you have done a King Alfred and burnt it. A quick test for doneness is to insert a metal skewer and if it comes out clean the cake is cooked. Leave to cool in the tin for 5 minutes, then turn it out onto a wire rack. Serve warm with ice cream – yum, yum – or leave it to cool and enjoy with a nice cup of tea.

HAIRY BIKERS' STOLLEN

Germans make good cars and they also make tasty cake so give this a shot – it's a great alternative to Christmas cake. This is like the richest, spiciest fruit loaf you've ever tasted, bursting with fruit and nuts and a nugget of marzipan in every slice.

MAKES 1 BIG STOLLEN

500g strong white bread flour
2 tsp fast-action dried yeast
1 large free-range egg
100g butter
150g golden caster sugar
225g warm milk
½ tsp salt
50g sultanas
50g currants
100g mixed peel
50g flaked almonds
50g walnuts, roughly chopped
100g glacé cherries, halved
1½ tsp ground ginger
2 tsp mixed spice
1 tsp cinnamon
270g good marzipan (see page 72)
vanilla sugar and cinnamon

First make the dough. Place the flour, dried yeast, egg, butter, caster sugar, milk and salt in a bowl and knead until you have a soft but elastic dough. You can do this in a mixer with a dough hook if you prefer. Carefully fold in the sultanas, currants, mixed peel, almonds, walnuts, cherries, ginger, mixed spice and cinnamon. Cover the bowl with clingfilm and leave the dough to double in size for at least an hour.

Put the dough onto a work surface, knock it back and flatten it out. Shape the marzipan into a sausage and place this onto the dough. Fold the dough over the marzipan and shape into a loaf. Cover and leave to rise again for about 45 minutes. Preheat the oven to 180°C/Gas 4.

Place on a greased baking sheet, join side down. Bake in the preheated oven for 35–40 minutes, then cool on a wire rack. Finish with a sprinkling of vanilla sugar and cinnamon.

OLD-FASHIONED MINCE PIES
WITH AN ORANGE CRUST

These mince pies are wonderfully boozy and spicy with a delicious orange pastry – guaranteed to bring a smile even to Ebenezer Scrooge! Ideally, make the mincemeat the day before so the flavours can mature and the pies will taste even better. The mincemeat recipe makes enough for two batches of mince pies.

MAKES 18 MINCE PIES

MINCEMEAT
1 lemon, boiled for 1 hour until soft and left to cool
200g raisins
200g sultanas
1 Bramley cooking apple, peeled and chopped
200g dried mixed fruit
150g mixed peel
200g suet
200g dark brown muscovado sugar
200g currants
1 tsp cinnamon
½ tsp grated nutmeg
2 tsp mixed spice
½ tsp ground ginger
100ml brandy
100ml sherry

ORANGE SHORTCRUST PASTRY
450g plain flour
1 tsp baking powder
1 tbsp caster sugar
½ tsp salt
120g unsalted butter, cold, plus extra for greasing the tins
zest of 2 oranges
140ml orange juice
1 free-range egg, beaten

First make the mincemeat. Cut the cooled boiled lemon in half and take out all the pips. Place it in a food processor and add the raisins, sultanas, apple, mixed fruit and mixed peel. Blitz to a paste. Turn this out into a bowl and add the suet, sugar, currants, cinnamon, nutmeg, mixed spice, ground ginger, brandy and sherry. Mix together well and set aside. This mincemeat can be stored in a dark, cool cupboard and keeps well for up to a year.

To make the pastry, tip the flour into a food processor, add the baking powder, sugar, salt and butter, then blitz until the mixture has a crumb-like texture. Add the orange zest, then gradually add the orange juice and process until the pastry forms a ball. Wrap the pastry in clingfilm and set aside in the fridge to chill.

Preheat the oven to 200°C/Gas 6 and grease the mince pie tins. Roll out half the pastry and cut out rounds for the bottom of the pies. Place these into their little nests in the tins. Add a good dessertspoon of mincemeat to each. Roll out the remaining pastry and, using a smaller pastry cutter, cut out rounds for the lids. Brush the tops with beaten egg and cut a steam hole in each pie with a sharp knife. Bake in the preheated oven for about 20 minutes until golden. Great with whipped cream, brandy butter (see page 120) or ice cream.

CHOCOLATE YULE LOG

This deliciously moist sponge has a creamy, coffee-flavoured centre and a rich chocolate coating.

SERVES 8–10

soft butter for greasing
6 large free-range eggs, separated
150g caster sugar
50g cocoa powder

ICING AND FILLING
200g plain, dark chocolate,
broken into squares
200g icing sugar
200g butter, room temperature
2 tbsp Camp chicory and coffee essence

DECORATION
icing sugar or desiccated coconut

Preheat the oven to 180°C/Gas 4. Line a 23 x 33cm Swiss roll tin with baking parchment, grease with a little butter and set aside.

Put the egg yolks and sugar in a large bowl and beat with an electric whisk until thick and creamy. Sift the cocoa powder over the egg mixture and whisk in thoroughly. Wash and dry the beaters and whisk the egg whites until stiff but not dry. Fold a third of the egg whites into the cocoa mixture, then gently fold in the rest until evenly distributed. Pour the mixture into the tin and spread gently with a spatula. Bake for 20–25 minutes or until well risen and beginning to shrink away from the sides of the tin.

Remove the cake from the oven, loosen the edges with a round-bladed knife and leave to stand for a few minutes. Place a piece of baking parchment on the work surface, turn the cake out onto the parchment and leave it to cool for 30–40 minutes.

Meanwhile, make the icing. Melt the chocolate in a heatproof bowl over a pan of simmering water, or in a microwave oven. Remove from the heat and leave to cool, but do not allow it to set. Put the icing sugar in a food processor, add the butter and blitz until smooth. Add the coffee essence and 2 tablespoons of melted chocolate, then blend until smooth. Make sure the chocolate is cool, or it will melt the butter.

Take just over half the icing mixture out of the processor and put it in a bowl to use for the filling. With the motor running, slowly add the remaining chocolate to the icing mixture in the processor and blend until smooth. This will be used for icing the cake.

When the cake is cool, trim off the crusty edges. Using a palette knife or spatula, spread the filling over the cake, taking it right to the edges. Starting at one of the long sides, gently roll up the sponge, keeping the first roll fairly tight so it forms a good spiral shape. Spread the icing evenly over the cake and drag a fork through it to resemble the ridges on the bark of a tree. Chill for at least 30 minutes to allow the icing to set. Decorate with sifted icing sugar or desiccated coconut.

Cut a thick diagonal slice, about 8cm long, off one end of the roll and use some icing to attach this to one side of the cake to resemble a stump.

LEBKUCHEN

These are traditional German-style Christmas biscuits. You can make them into lovely little edible tree decorations by making a hole at the top of each one during the baking process.

MAKES 24

75g butter
150ml runny honey
50g soft dark brown sugar
finely grated zest of 1 unwaxed lemon
finely grated zest of 1 well-washed orange
225g plain flour
75g ground almonds
2 tsp ground ginger
1 heaped tsp ground cinnamon
½ heaped tsp ground allspice
½ heaped tsp freshly grated nutmeg
1 tsp baking powder
½ tsp bicarbonate of soda

ICING
100g icing sugar
3 tbsp egg white, lightly beaten with a whisk

Put the butter in a saucepan with the honey, brown sugar and lemon and orange zest. Place over a low heat until the butter melts, stirring occasionally. While the butter is melting, sift the flour into a large bowl and stir in the almonds, ginger, cinnamon, allspice, nutmeg, baking powder and bicarbonate of soda. Pour the honey mixture into the dry ingredients and stir with a wooden spoon to make a fairly stiff dough.

Preheat the oven to 180°C/Gas 4. Put the dough on a board and cut it into quarters. Cut each quarter into 6 and roll the pieces into small, neat balls with your hands.

Line 2 large baking trays with baking parchment and place the balls of dough onto them, leaving room between each one as they will spread. Flatten the balls with your fingertips so they are about 5mm high. Cut them into pretty shapes if you wish.

Bake for 10–12 minutes until the biscuits are firm and lightly browned. The longer the biscuits are cooked the crisper they will become, but bear in mind that traditional lebkuchen are quite soft. Transfer the biscuits to a rack and leave to cool. If you want to make lebkuchen to hang on your Christmas tree, take the biscuits out of the oven after 8–10 minutes and carefully make a hole at the top of each one with a skewer. Put them back in the oven for a few more minutes.

To make the icing, sift the icing sugar into a bowl and stir in the egg white, a little at a time, to form a smooth, fairly runny icing. Drop a teaspoon of the icing onto each biscuit and spread it with the back of the spoon until evenly covered. Leave the icing to dry for several hours or overnight. Store the biscuits in an airtight container or hang them on your Christmas tree. The biscuits are best eaten within 5 days.

WHITE CHOCOLATE & SOUR CHERRY CHEESECAKE

This is so good it's sex on a plate – a real grown-up cake, so put the kids to bed and indulge yourselves. You deserve a treat after all that Christmas shopping.

SERVES 8–10

BASE
vegetable oil for greasing
200g chocolate digestive biscuits, roughly broken up
75g butter

FILLING
150g white chocolate, broken into squares
600g full-fat soft cheese
150ml double cream
175g caster sugar
2 large free-range egg yolks
4 large free-range eggs

CHERRY SAUCE
150g dried sour cherries
100ml cherry brandy
3 tbsp morello cherry jam
2 tsp ground arrowroot

Oil a 23cm springform cake tin and line the base with baking parchment. Pulse the biscuits to crumbs in a food processor. Melt the butter in a small pan and pour it into the processor with the motor running. Blend until the biscuits and butter are thoroughly combined. Spread this mixture evenly over the base of the tin, pressing it down lightly. Leave to set in the fridge.

Melt the chocolate in a heatproof bowl over a pan of simmering water. Leave to cool for 20 minutes, but do not allow it to set. Preheat the oven to 180°C/Gas 4. Put the cheese, cream, sugar, egg yolks and eggs in a food processor and blend until smooth. With the motor running, gradually add the cooled chocolate and blend until just mixed. Pour the mixture onto the biscuit base.

Put a large piece of foil on the work surface. Place the tin in the centre of the foil and bring up the sides of the foil to protect the cheesecake while it cooks. Place the tin in a roasting tray and add enough just-boiled water to come about 2cm up the sides of the cake tin. Carefully place the roasting tin in the centre of the oven and bake for 45–50 minutes. The cheesecake is ready when it is almost, but not fully, set. Jiggle the tin and you should see the filling ripple under the surface.

To make the sauce, put the cherries and cherry brandy in a pan with 100ml of water and bring to a gentle simmer. Cook for 5 minutes, stirring occasionally. Add the jam and cook for 1 minute more. Mix the arrowroot with a tablespoon of water in a bowl and stir it into the sauce. Cook over a low heat for 2–3 minutes until the sauce is thick and glossy. Pour into a heatproof jug and leave to cool, then cover and chill.

When the cheesecake is ready, turn off the oven but leave the cake inside for a further 30 minutes. This helps prevent the surface cracking as the cheesecake cools. Lift the cake tin from the water and remove the foil. Chill the cheesecake in the fridge for at least 2 hours before serving with the cherry sauce.

HOME-MADE MARZIPAN

You can buy marzipan of course, but our home-made version is much better so give your Christmas cake a treat. Please note: this recipe contains raw eggs.

MAKES ENOUGH FOR 20–23CM ROUND OR 20CM SQUARE CAKE

225g icing sugar, plus at least 3 tbsp for rolling
350g ground almonds
175g caster sugar
2 large free-range eggs
½ tsp almond extract
1 tsp freshly squeezed lemon juice

FOR DECORATING THE CAKE
icing sugar
1 egg white
or 100g apricot jam
ready-roll white icing

Sift the 225g icing sugar into a large bowl and stir in the almonds and caster sugar. Beat the eggs with the almond extract and lemon juice. Using a large spoon, stir the eggs into the almonds and sugar until the mixture begins to come together. Now use your hands to continue combining the mixture into a stiff but pliable paste.

Dust the work surface with some sifted icing sugar and knead the marzipan for a minute or two until it is smooth. Put it back into the bowl, cover with clingfilm and leave to stand for 1–2 hours before using. This allows the almonds to swell and absorb some of the moisture from the egg mixture.

When you're ready to decorate your cake, roll the marzipan out on a surface heavily dusted with icing sugar. Brush the top and sides of the cake with egg white or warmed apricot jam, then cut a piece of marzipan to fit the top of the cake. Press it into place, then cut strips to go round the sides of the cake. Press the pieces of marzipan together at the joins. Leave the marzipan to dry for a few days before adding icing. We're happy to use ready-roll white icing on our Christmas cakes – leaves more time for decorating!

Christmas
Eve
∞

COARSE COUNTRY TERRINE

This is best made the day before you need it and is delicious served in thick slices with lots of hot, crusty bread and butter or melba toast. Perfect with our Christmas chutney (see page 29).

SERVES 10

300g rindless pork shoulder
300g rindless pork belly
150g unsmoked streaky bacon rashers, rinds removed
225g pig's liver, rinsed and patted dry
2 garlic cloves, peeled and crushed
freshly squeezed juice and finely grated zest of 1 orange
6 tbsp brandy
3 tbsp finely chopped fresh sage leaves
1 tbsp finely chopped fresh thyme leaves
1 tbsp whole black peppercorns
1 tbsp juniper berries
400g smoked streaky bacon rashers, rinds removed
200g jar of cornichons (extra small gherkins), drained (about 40g cornichons)
sea salt and freshly ground black pepper

This is one recipe where thin supermarket streaky bacon works really well, as it can be stretched easily with the back of a knife. Use a double layer of cornichons for extra colour and a crunchy texture if you like.

Cut the pork shoulder, belly and unsmoked bacon into small pieces, discarding any tough fat, rind or sinew. Put half the meats with the liver and garlic in a food processor and blend until smooth. Add the rest of the meat and pulse until roughly chopped and well mixed with the puréed meat. Tip into a bowl and stir in the juice, zest, brandy and herbs. Grind the peppercorns and juniper berries with a pestle and mortar, then add them to the mixture. Stir well. Cover the bowl with clingfilm and leave in the fridge for 1–3 hours to marinate.

Place the smoked rashers on a board and stretch them with the back of a knife. Use these to line a 1-litre lidded terrine or ovenproof dish. Place the first rasher diagonally across the dish, allowing one end of the rasher to overlap the side of the dish by about 5cm – these ends will be folded over the top of the terrine. Put the second rasher across the first, starting at the opposite corner. Work your way down the dish, crossing the bacon rashers from one side to the other. Use halved rashers of bacon to line the dish at each end.

Preheat the oven to 170°C/Gas 3. Spoon half the meat mixture into the lined terrine and place the cornichons neatly down the centre. Spoon the rest of the meat on top of the cornichons and smooth the surface firmly. Fold the bacon overlapping the sides of the dish up and over the meat to cover.

Put the lid on or cover with foil and place the terrine in a roasting tin. Add enough just-boiled water to come 2cm up the outside of the dish and bake in the centre of the oven for 1½ hours. Remove the terrine from the oven and insert a skewer into the centre. Hold for 10 seconds, then take it out. If the terrine is done the skewer should feel hot. The terrine should also have shrunk away from the sides of the dish. Take the dish out of the roasting tin and cover the terrine with a double layer of foil. Put a couple of cans or other weights on top and leave to cool, then chill in the fridge overnight. Next day, turn the terrine out onto a board and cut into thick slices.

SI'S MUSSELS
WITH COGNAC & CREAM

This recipe is a bit of a tradition in the King household on Christmas Eve. It's an eagerly awaited event every year and our middle son James always insists on preparing and cooking the mussels. Make sure you get your fair share – somehow I always seem to get a small portion.

SERVES 4–6

2kg mussels
50g unsalted butter
4 shallots, finely chopped
1 garlic clove, finely chopped
50ml dry white wine
1 tbsp chopped fresh thyme
1 bay leaf
2 tbsp finely chopped parsley
2 tsp freshly ground black pepper
1 tbsp brandy
50ml single cream
(or double if you prefer)

Wash the mussels under running water. Remove all traces of mud, seaweed and barnacles with a blunt knife or hard brush. Pull off the beards – the hairy bits poking out of the shells – and discard any mussels with cracked or broken shells. If any mussel is slightly open, tap the shell sharply and if it doesn't close, chuck it out. Once all the mussels are cleaned and checked, rinse them again under running water. It is possible to buy ready-cleaned mussels if you want, so ask your fishmonger or supermarket if they have any available.

You need a large pan with a lid. Melt the butter in the pan and gently sauté the shallots and garlic until transparent but not coloured. This should take about 5 minutes. Add the wine, thyme, bay leaf, half the parsley and the pepper and increase the heat to bring the liquid to the boil.

Pile in the mussels, put the lid on the pan and steam them over a high heat for about 2 minutes. Turn the mussels over with a large spoon or spatula, add the brandy and cook for another 3 minutes or so or until the shells have opened. If any of the mussels do not open after cooking, chuck them out. Add the cream and the rest of the parsley and stir through the mussels.

Serve immediately with hot baguettes for dipping in the juices and a glass of Normandy cider as a Christmas Eve tipple!

DAVE'S SPATCHCOCKED DUCK

This is a great festive treat and my traditional Christmas Eve supper. Spatchcocking ensures that the meat cooks evenly and you get loads of crispy skin – it's more flat duck than Fat Duck! Serve with any of the normal trimmings but if you are saving yourself for the big day, how about just a nice green salad, potato salad and some crusty bread.

SERVES 2–4

1 fat duck
2 tbsp olive oil
1 tbsp sea salt flakes
1 tsp cracked black pepper
1 tbsp honey
1 tbsp treacle
2 tbsp orange juice

Weigh the duck so you can work out the cooking time and then place it on its front so it is breast side down. Take a pair of boning shears or a stout knife and remove the backbone – basically, find the neck and chop away either side down to the duck's bum. Turn the bird over and press it down with your hands until it is as flat as possible. Rub the skin of the duck all over with the olive oil, then rub in the sea salt flakes and cracked pepper. Keep the backbone to chuck into your turkey gravy stockpot on Christmas Day.

Preheat the oven to 190°C/Gas 5. Place the duck, breast side up now, on a rack above a roasting tin and roast in the preheated oven for 20 minutes per 500g. Then turn the oven up as high as it will go, say 230°C/Gas 8, and cook for 15 minutes more to crisp up the skin.

Mix the honey, treacle and orange juice. Paint this mixture over the duck and put it back into the oven for another 5 minutes to give it a lovely glaze. You can do this under a grill if you prefer.

Place the duck in the middle of your table for everyone to help themselves – it's a bit like tear-and-share bread but with a quack!

The roasting tin will be full of gorgeous duck fat. Please, please keep this to roast your potatoes in on Christmas Day.

STUFFED CHICKEN BREASTS
WITH POTATO ROSTI CAKES

Cumbria meets Umbria – our version of fusion food. These tasty chicken parcels
are great with potato rosti cakes and a simple salad on the side.

SERVES 4

4 plump free-range chicken breasts
175g Cumberland sausage meat
8 basil leaves
4 pieces of sundried tomato
150g (8 slices) Cumbrian air-dried ham
(Parma or any other kind will do)
1 tbsp olive oil
½ lemon
sea salt flakes
freshly ground black pepper

POTATO ROSTI CAKES
500g potatoes, peeled and grated
½ onion, peeled and grated
50g melted butter
sea salt flakes
freshly ground black pepper

Preheat the oven to 180°C/Gas 4. Take the chicken breasts
and cut a pocket into each one. Stuff a quarter of the sausage
meat into each pocket, then press in 2 basil leaves and a piece
of sundried tomato. Season with sea salt and black pepper.

Lay 2 pieces of ham side by side, overlapping them slightly.
Place a chicken breast on top, next to the edge closest to you.
Drizzle some oil over it, season and add a squeeze of lemon
juice. Roll the chicken up in its ham blanket to form a neat
roll and repeat until you have 4 lovely tucked-up bundles.
Wrap each one in foil and seal the parcels tightly. Put them
on an oven tray and bake in the preheated oven for 30 minutes.
Meanwhile, make the rosti cakes.

When the chicken is done, unwrap the foil, slice the breasts
and serve them with the rosti cakes. Add the juices from the foil
parcels as gravy if you like.

POTATO ROSTI CAKES
Mix the grated raw potato and onion and season well. Place the
mixture in a tea towel and squeeze out all the moisture. Lightly
grease a frying pan and 4 chef's rings with the melted butter,
then put the rings into the pan. Pack the potato mixture into
the rings and place the pan on the heat. Cook slowly for about
10 minutes on one side, then turn over and cook on the other
side until golden and cooked through.

Chef's rings, also called rosti rings or presentation rings, are
simple metal rings that help keep food such as rosti cakes neat
while cooking. They're available from kitchen shops.

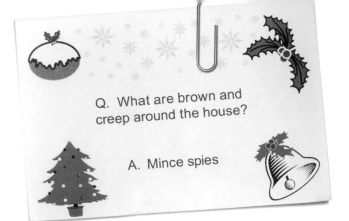

TRANSYLVANIAN TERRINE

Lili, Dave's wife, is from northern Transylvania where this dish is a Christmas Eve tradition. It's a wonderful jellied terrine, made from pigs' trotters, carrots and garlic, and is a truly great supper. You need to start this the day before so the liquid has plenty of time to set.

SERVES 8

4 pigs' trotters, sliced in half lengthways
12 black peppercorns
1 tsp sea salt flakes
3 carrots, peeled, topped and tailed
5 garlic cloves, crushed
freshly ground black pepper
1 tsp good paprika
lemon juice

Put the trotters in a large pan with 5 litres of water, bring to the boil and continue to boil slowly for 3½–4 hours.

Add the peppercorns, half the salt, the whole carrots and 3 of the crushed garlic cloves, then continue to boil for another hour. By now the broth should be reduced to about 1.5 litres

Drain the contents of the pan into a colander set over a bowl and reserve the cooking liquor. Leave the trotters to rest and cool. When they are cold, pick the meat off the bones, dice it and arrange it evenly over the bottom of a square pie dish or roasting tin. The layer should be about 2cm thick. Slice the cold carrots into thin discs and arrange them neatly over the meat.

Return the cooking liquor to the pan and bring it to the boil. Add the rest of the salt, crushed garlic and some ground black pepper to taste, then leave it to simmer gently for half an hour. Pour this liquid over the diced meat and carrots.

Mix a teaspoon of ground black pepper with a teaspoon of paprika. Using a sieve, sprinkle this evenly over the liquid – just like you would sprinkle icing sugar onto a cake – so the surface looks red.

Cover the dish with foil and leave it to rest in a cool place or in the fridge until the next day when it will be nicely set. Cut it in neat squares and serve with a squeeze of lemon juice on top. Great served with crusty brown bread and dill pickles.

BEST-EVER MULLED WINE

SERVES 12

4 tangerines, clementines or satsumas
1 vanilla pod, split lengthways
8 cloves and 8 allspice berries
2 cinnamon sticks
3 star anise
3 bay leaves
300g caster sugar
2 x 75cl bottles of red wine
200ml brandy

Cut the tangerines into 4 or 5 thick slices and put them in a large saucepan. Add the vanilla pod, cloves, allspice, cinnamon, star anise and bay leaves. Stir in the sugar. Pour over the wine and brandy and place the pan over a low heat. Bring to a gentle simmer and bubble over a very low heat for 15 minutes, stirring occasionally.

Remove the pan from the heat and set aside for 1–4 hours before serving to allow the flavours to blend. Heat through gently without boiling, then strain, leaving some of the larger spices for decoration, and ladle into heatproof cups.

CREAMY EGG NOG

SERVES 8–10

4 free-range eggs, separated
100g caster sugar
500ml whole milk
450ml double cream
150ml Bourbon or whisky
50ml dark rum
50ml brandy
finely grated nutmeg

Note: this recipe contains raw eggs. Whisk the egg yolks and sugar in a large bowl until thick and pale – the whisk should leave a trail of mixture when lifted from the bowl. Whisk in the milk and 300ml of the cream, followed by the Bourbon, rum and brandy. Cover and leave the mixture in the fridge for at least 6 hours or overnight. Store the egg whites in a separate bowl, covered, in the fridge until ready to use.

Just before serving, whisk the egg whites until stiff but not dry and fold them into the yolk mixture. Whisk the remaining cream until soft peaks form and fold this into the egg mixture. Using a large metal whisk, gently break up any lumpy bits of egg white. Pour the mixture into a large jug and sprinkle with grated nutmeg. Serve cold.

ROYAL GIN FIZZ

SERVES 4

100ml Genever gin (or London will do)
2 dsrtsp caster sugar
1 free-range egg white
juice of 1 lemon
1 bottle champagne (or cheap fizz)

Note: this recipe contains raw egg. Pour the gin into a blender and add the sugar, egg white, lemon juice and a couple of handfuls of ice. Blitz, then pour into 4 highball glasses or tumblers. Top up with champagne and raise your glasses – guaranteed to cheer up the in-laws!

COFFEE CARDAMOM ZABAGLIONE
WITH AFFOGATO

This is a really classy pud, with wonderful contrasts of texture, temperature and flavour. And the shot of espresso is guaranteed to perk you up after dinner. Affogato means drowned in Italian – you 'drown' the ice cream in piping-hot coffee.

SERVES 4

8 cardamom pods
8 free-range egg yolks
50g golden caster sugar
2 tbsp cold strong espresso coffee
4 tbsp Tia Maria

AFFOGATO
4 scoops of good vanilla ice cream
4 shots of hot espresso coffee
dark chocolate shavings

Remove the shells from the cardamom pods and crush the black seeds in a pestle and mortar. Put the egg yolks in a bowl with the sugar and add the cardamom seeds. Using an electric hand whisk, beat for a couple of minutes until the mixture is pale and creamy. Whisk in the cold coffee and Tia Maria.

Pour the mixture into a heatproof bowl and set it over a pan of hot water. Place the pan on a low heat and whisk the mixture for about 10 minutes until it thickens and doubles in volume. Don't let the water in the pan boil or the zabaglione will curdle.

Take 4 nice glasses, place a scoop of ice cream in each and add a shot of hot espresso. Spoon the zabaglione on top and sprinkle with shavings of dark chocolate. Serve at once.

Christmas
Day

Christmas countdown

There's nothing that difficult about cooking Christmas dinner – it's just that there's a lot of it. Getting the timing right so that everything is ready when you need it is the hard part and that's what we're here to help with. This is the order of events that works for us for getting a 6kg turkey and all the trimmings on the table at 2.30pm. It's easy enough to adjust the timings if you want to eat earlier or later. And if you want a starter, serve something such as pâté or soup that can be prepared in advance. The turkey will keep warm for up to an hour if necessary. Think of it as a big Sunday lunch and let's get started.

Christmas Eve

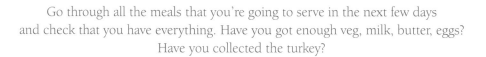

Go through all the meals that you're going to serve in the next few days
and check that you have everything. Have you got enough veg, milk, butter, eggs?
Have you collected the turkey?

Take the giblets out of your turkey and make the stock (see page 108).

Blitz some white bread to make crumbs for your bread sauce and stuffing and
store them in a plastic bag in the fridge. You can make the stuffing too
if you like (see page 109), but don't add the eggs until just before you stuff the turkey.

Make the cranberry sauce (see page 112).

Make the brandy butter for the pud (see page 120). Store in the fridge.

Peel and trim the sprouts and put them in a bag in the fridge.

If you're serving bacon-wrapped chipolatas (see page 119), you can get these
ready too and keep them stashed away in the fridge, ready to be cooked.

Before you go to bed, take the turkey out of the fridge and leave it somewhere safe
(well away from the cat) so it has a chance to come to room temperature.

Christmas Day

9.30am
Put the oven on at 190°C/Gas 5 so it can heat up while you finish the stuffings for the turkey.

10am
Stuff the turkey and put it in the oven (see our timings on page 108).

10.30am
Prepare the spiced milk for the bread sauce so it has plenty of time to infuse (see page 119).

Peel all the potatoes, parsnips, etc. Put them in pans of cold water.

Put your feet up while someone else clears up the mess so far. Sherry time!

11am
Give the turkey a quick check. Make the brandy cream if serving.

1.15pm
Parboil the potatoes and drain, ready for roasting.

1.30pm
Put some goose fat, dripping or oil in a roasting tin and pop it in the oven to heat up, ready for cooking the potatoes (see page 112). Heat some oil or fat in another tin for your parsnips (see page 113) and put them in the oven.

Check the turkey just in case it's done already (see pages 108–109).

Blanch the sprouts, ready to be finished off with pancetta and chestnuts (see page 112).

1.45pm
Dredge the parboiled potatoes with polenta. Take the pan of fat out of the oven, add the potatoes and put them in the oven. Finish the bread sauce and any other veg.

Get someone to set the table. Beer time!

1.50pm
Put your Christmas pudding on to steam.

Check the turkey – it should be ready. Take it out of the oven, cover it with foil and a tea towel and leave to rest. Turn the oven up to finish cooking the potatoes and parsnips.

If you're serving chipolatas in bacon, put them in the oven now.

Very important – make the gravy.

Make sure you have plenty of serving dishes, plates and a gravy jug warm and ready.

2.15pm
Check the potatoes and parsnips. Take the parsnips out of the oven, add honey or maple syrup (see page 113) and put them back in the oven for 10 minutes.

Fry the pancetta for the sprouts and warm everything through.

2.30pm
Proudly carry your beautiful turkey to the table and get the carver started while you serve all the accompaniments. Bring the hot gravy at the last minute, then relax and enjoy yourself. Posh wine time!

4pm
The pudding should be ready. Turn off the heat and leave it to sit in the steamer until you're ready to eat. It will keep hot for a while, so don't feel you have to rush. Don't forget to serve the brandy butter or other sauces. Christmas pudding vodka time!

JERUSALEM ARTICHOKE SOUP
WITH BACON & PARSLEY CROUTONS

This is a warm, velvety soup that's packed with flavour. If you prefer a vegetarian version,
use a vegetable stock cube and leave the bacon out of the croutons.

SERVES 4–6

50g butter
1 tbsp sunflower oil
1 large onion, roughly chopped
1kg Jerusalem artichokes
1 garlic clove, crushed
800ml chicken stock, fresh or cube
150ml milk
3 tbsp double cream (optional)
sea salt flakes
freshly ground black pepper

CROUTONS
3 tbsp sunflower oil
2 thick slices of white bread, crusts
removed
3 rindless smoked streaky bacon rashers,
cut into 1cm pieces
2 tbsp finely chopped parsley

Melt the butter in a large saucepan with the oil. Gently fry the onion for 10 minutes, until it is very soft, stirring occasionally. While the onion is cooking, peel the artichokes and cut them into small cubes.

Add the artichokes and garlic to the onion, cover the pan with a tight-fitting lid and cook over a low heat for 10 minutes, stirring occasionally, until the artichokes begin to soften. Don't let them brown. Pour the stock into the pan, add a few pinches of salt and twists of black pepper. Bring to the boil, put the lid on the pan and simmer gently for 35–40 minutes or until the artichokes are soft. Give the soup a stir every now and then.

While the soup is simmering, prepare the garnish. Heat 2½ tablespoons of the oil in a small non-stick frying pan. Cut the bread into small cubes and add them to the pan. Cook over a low to medium heat for 3–4 minutes, turning regularly, until the cubes are golden brown on all sides. Tip them into a bowl and return the pan to the heat.

Pour the remaining oil into the pan and add the bacon. Fry for 2–3 minutes, stirring occasionally, until the bacon fat is golden and crisp. Put the cubes of bread back in the pan and toss them with the bacon for a minute or so. Set aside.

Remove the soup from the heat and leave it to stand for 10 minutes. Then pour the soup into a food processor or blender. Add the milk and blend until it is as smooth and velvety as possible. Pour the soup back into the pan and adjust the seasoning to taste. Add cream for a slightly richer soup, or a little more milk if the soup appears too thick. Warm through gently, stirring regularly.

Warm the bacon croutons over a low heat and stir in the chopped parsley. Ladle the soup into warmed bowls and sprinkle with the croutons to serve.

POTTED SMOKED MACKEREL PÂTÉ

This creamy smoked mackerel pâté, topped with clarified butter, makes a perfect starter before your big Christmas dinner or can be served with bread and salad as a light lunch on other days. Cheap to make, it has a million-dollar taste. If you prefer a coarser pâté, simply mix the onion juice, cheese, horseradish, lemon zest and juice in a bowl until smooth, then add the flaked mackerel and mash with a fork until it reaches a consistency you like. You need six to eight 125ml ramekin dishes.

SERVES 6–8

300g smoked mackerel fillets, skinned
½ small onion
200g full-fat soft cheese
2 tbsp creamed horseradish sauce
finely grated zest and juice of
½ unwaxed lemon
sea salt flakes
freshly ground black pepper
warm crusty granary bread or melba toast

TOPPING
100g butter
6–8 small bay leaves
½ tbsp mixed dried peppercorns,
miniature capers or
pickled green peppercorns

Flake the mackerel into a food processor. Peel the onion and grate it coarsely onto a plate. Take the grated onion in one hand and squeeze it hard over the mackerel to release the juice – this will add flavour to the pâté. Discard the onion flesh.

Add the soft cheese, horseradish sauce, lemon zest and juice to the mackerel and season well with a good pinch of salt and plenty of freshly ground black pepper. Blitz all the ingredients together until smooth. Check the seasoning and add a little more lemon juice if needed. Spoon the mixture into the ramekins and smooth the tops with the back of a teaspoon.

To make the clarified butter topping, melt the butter in a small pan over a very low heat. Remove from the heat, pour the butter into a jug and spoon off any foam that rises to the surface. Leave to stand for a few minutes to allow the milk solids to sink to the bottom of the jug.

When the butter is looking clear, pour a tablespoon over the pâté in each ramekin. Place a bay leaf and a few peppercorns on top, cover with clingfilm and leave in the fridge to set. Best eaten within 2–3 days.

To serve, take the ramekins out of the fridge about 20 minutes before eating. Put them on small plates with warm bread or melba toast and serve while the bread remains hot enough to melt the clarified butter. There is no need to serve extra butter at the table.

GOAT CHEESE SALAD
WITH HONEY & MUSTARD DRESSING

This fresh-tasting salad makes a great starter for your Christmas meal. The mild honey and mustard dressing goes perfectly with the tanginess of the goat cheese.

SERVES 4–6

4 slices of fresh white bread
1–2 tsp hazelnut or walnut oil, for drizzling
2 x 110g goat cheese logs
50g blanched hazelnuts (or walnut halves)
2 heads of chicory
(ideally the red ones), trimmed
50g bag of mixed spinach,
watercress and rocket salad
1 small red onion, peeled
2 beetroot (each about 65g), vacuum-
packed or freshly cooked and peeled
freshly ground black pepper

HONEY & MUSTARD DRESSING
1 tbsp white wine vinegar
1 tsp Dijon mustard
2 tsp runny honey
3 tbsp hazelnut or walnut oil
2 tbsp extra virgin olive oil
sea salt flakes
freshly ground black pepper

Toast the bread on both sides until golden. Cut each slice of toast into 3 discs, using a 5cm biscuit cutter. You'll need 12 discs of roughly the same diameter as the cheese or slightly larger. Place the toasts on a baking tray and drizzle with a little of the oil. Trim the ends off the cheese and cut each log into 6 even slices. Place one on top of each toast and season with a little ground black pepper.

Cut the hazelnuts in half or break the walnuts into 2 or 3 pieces. Put the nuts in a dry frying pan and toast them over a medium heat, turning regularly, until golden. Remove from the heat.

Separate the chicory into leaves and rinse well. Pat them dry with a clean tea towel, or kitchen paper, and place on a large serving platter or individual plates. Add the mixed leaves and toss lightly together. Cut the onion into thin rings and scatter these over the leaves. Quarter the beetroot and arrange them on top of the salad.

To make the dressing, whisk the vinegar, mustard, honey, salt and a few twists of ground black pepper in a bowl with a large balloon whisk until well mixed. Gradually add the oils, whisking constantly until thick. Check the seasoning.

When ready to serve, preheat the grill to hot. Place the cheese toasts under the grill and cook for 1–2 minutes until the cheese is softened and beginning to brown. Remove from the heat and put them on the salad, using a palette knife. Scatter with the toasted nuts and drizzle with the honey and mustard dressing. Serve immediately while the cheese is hot.

LEMON & PARSLEY ROASTED SALMON
WITH CHAMPAGNE & CHIVE SAUCE

A stunning centrepiece, this is roasted in just 40 minutes and is dead easy to serve. You can get everything ready in advance and keep it in the fridge until ready to cook. Ask your fishmonger to zscale and fillet a whole salmon into two sides. Use tweezers to remove any stubborn little pin bones.

SERVES 6–8

2 x 750g fresh salmon fillets, scaled and pin boned
freshly ground black pepper
1 unwaxed lemon, sliced
6–8 bay leaves
3 tbsp olive oil

LEMON & PARSLEY STUFFING
25g butter
1 tbsp olive oil
1 medium onion, finely chopped
1 large garlic clove, finely diced
3 celery sticks, trimmed and finely diced
juice and finely grated zest of 1 unwaxed lemon
300g fresh white breadcrumbs
1 large bunch of fresh curly parsley, stalks removed, leaves finely chopped (you'll need at least 7–8 tbsp)
sea salt flakes
freshly ground black pepper

CHAMPAGNE & CHIVE SAUCE
15g butter
½ small onion, finely chopped
1 garlic clove, crushed
500ml champagne, cava or sparkling wine, plus an extra 2–3 tbsp
½ tsp caster sugar
300ml double cream
3 tbsp finely chopped fresh chives
sea salt flakes
freshly ground black pepper

To make the stuffing, melt the butter with the oil in a frying pan. Add the onion, garlic and celery and cook for 8–10 minutes until softened, but not coloured, stirring regularly. Add the juice, zest and breadcrumbs and season. Continue cooking, stirring constantly, for 5–6 minutes until the breadcrumbs are lightly browned in places. Tip into a bowl, stir in the parsley and leave to cool. Preheat the oven to 200°C/Gas 6.

Place one salmon side on a board, skin side down. Cut 6–8 pieces of kitchen string, each about 12cm long. Slide the string under the salmon, spacing the pieces closely for 8 servings and farther apart for 6 servings. Season the salmon with black pepper. Spoon the stuffing along the length of the salmon and press it down lightly. Season the second fillet and place it on top of the stuffing, skin side up. Bring the centre string up around the salmon, place a slice of lemon and a bay leaf on the salmon and knot the string around them. Tie the rest in the same way. Spread a piece of foil onto a baking tray. Gently place the stuffed salmon diagonally on top and bring up the foil around the sides. Drizzle the salmon with olive oil and season. Bake the fish for 20 minutes. Remove from the oven, spoon any juices in the foil over the salmon and return to the oven for another 20 minutes.

Meanwhile, prepare the sauce. Melt the butter in a pan and gently fry the onion and garlic for 5 minutes or until soft but not coloured. Pour the champagne into the pan and bring to the boil. Cook for 4–5 minutes or until the liquid is reduced by half. Stir in the sugar and cream and return to the boil. Cook for 2–3 minutes, stirring occasionally until the sauce coats the back of a spoon. Season, stir in the chives and set aside.

When the salmon is ready, snip off the string. Reheat the sauce. Cut the salmon into thick slices, each with lemon and bay leaf. Pour the 2–3 tablespoons of champagne into the hot sauce and let it fizz, then spoon a little of the foam over the salmon. Pour the rest of the sauce into a warmed jug and serve separately.

ROAST LOIN OF PORK
WITH PRUNE & APPLE STUFFING

A delicious, traditional recipe for roast pork with a tangy cider gravy. The fruity stuffing is a doddle to make and helps add flavour and sweetness to the gravy. Ideally, buy a good-sized piece of pork from the butcher, as the rind will almost certainly make better crackling. And if you're worried about scoring the rind or making a pocket for the stuffing, ask your butcher to do it for you.

SERVES 6

2 medium banana (long) shallots or
1 medium onion, sliced
2kg boned loin of pork, rind scored
thinly but deeply
1 tsp sea salt flakes, for the crackling

To make the stuffing, melt the butter with the oil in a large non-stick frying pan. Cook the chopped shallots and garlic over a low heat for about 10 minutes until softened and beginning to brown, stirring occasionally. Add the apple to the pan along with the lemon zest and prunes. Cook over a fairly high heat for 3–4 minutes until the apples begin to soften, stirring regularly. Stir in the honey and sage. Toss together for a couple of minutes until hot, then remove from the heat and stir in the breadcrumbs and plenty of seasoning. If you are not cooking the pork immediately, allow the stuffing to cool completely before using.

PRUNE & APPLE STUFFING

15g butter
1 tbsp sunflower oil
2 medium banana shallots or 1 medium onion, thinly sliced
2 garlic cloves, finely chopped
1 large Bramley apple, peeled, cored and cut into small chunks
finely grated zest of 1 unwaxed lemon
100g no-soak pitted prunes, quartered
1 tbsp clear honey
2 tsp dried sage or 2 tbsp finely shredded fresh sage leaves
50g fresh white breadcrumbs
sea salt flakes
freshly ground black pepper

CIDER GRAVY

2 tbsp plain flour
250ml dry cider
350ml vegetable cooking water
6–8 fresh sage leaves, finely shredded (optional)

If you like, add halved small apples to the tin for the last 20 minutes of the cooking time. Place them around the pork on the platter and serve in place of apple sauce. The little apples sold for kids' lunch boxes are ideal. You'll need half an apple per person.

Preheat the oven to 230°C/Gas 8. Place the sliced shallots, or onion, in a pile in the centre of a large, sturdy roasting tin – the heap should be about the same length as the pork. Put the pork on a board and pat the rind with kitchen paper to absorb any moisture. Cut off any string that may be holding it.

Cut between the eye of the meat and the rind, starting at the thin, rib end and working towards the centre. This is called 'seaming back' and you can ask your butcher to do it for you. Open out and spoon the stuffing evenly into the pocket made in the pork, leaving at least 2cm around the edge. Roll the meat up firmly, keeping the stuffing from bulging out of the pork. Cut about 5 pieces of kitchen string, 20cm long, and use them to tie the pork at even intervals – tie at each end and the middle first. Massage sea salt into the score marks made in the rind.

Place the pork on the bed of shallots and roast in the centre of the oven for 20 minutes. Turn the oven down to 190°C/Gas 5 and cook the pork for another hour. If any bits of the stuffing drop out onto the tray, try to scoop them up before they burn. They could make your gravy taste bitter. When the hour is up, take the pork out of the oven and transfer it to a baking tray. Turn the oven up to 230°C/Gas 8 and put the pork back in the oven for another 20 minutes, until the crackling is crisp.

To make the gravy, spoon off as much fat as possible from the original roasting tin, leaving all the softened shallots and flavoursome, sticky sediment. Throw away any burnt shallots. Place the tin on the hob, sprinkle over the flour and stir it into the pork juices. Pour over the cider and bring to the boil, stirring constantly. Cook for 2 minutes, then add the water and return to the boil. Leave to simmer for a few minutes, stirring occasionally, until all the sticky sediment has been scraped up from the bottom of the tin. Strain through a fine sieve into a saucepan and season to taste with salt and pepper. Set aside.

When the pork is ready, put it on a large, warmed serving platter, cover loosely with foil and leave it to rest for 15–20 minutes. Just before serving, warm the gravy until bubbling. Tip any pork resting juices into the gravy and heat through for a few minutes. Pour into a warmed gravy boat or jug, adding some shredded fresh sage leaves if you like. Carve the pork into thick slices and serve with the cider gravy and lots of mash and greens.

NUT & SPINACH ROAST
WITH WILD MUSHROOM GRAVY

This might sound like a bit of a cliché as a veggie option for Christmas Day, but if you're going to cook a nut roast, make it a good 'un. We reckon our version is tasty enough to make a carnivore turn. Try a slice with your turkey!

SERVES 4

200g fresh spinach leaves
250g unsalted mixed nuts
25g unsalted cashew nuts
½ onion, finely chopped
1 carrot, grated
200g canned tomatoes, drained and chopped
50g sundried tomatoes in olive oil, roughly chopped
1 free-range egg, beaten
100g Gruyère cheese, finely grated
½ tsp dried sage
½ tsp finely chopped fresh mint
1½ tbsp freshly chopped curly parsley
1 garlic clove, crushed
1 tsp vegetable stock concentrate
sea salt flakes
freshly ground black pepper
a knob of butter, for greasing tin

WILD MUSHROOM GRAVY

2 tbsp olive oil
a knob of butter
1 banana (long) shallot, finely diced
1 garlic clove, finely chopped
250g wild mushrooms
300ml vegetable stock
2 tbsp soy sauce
1 tbsp plain flour
1 tbsp butter
sea salt and black pepper

Preheat the oven to 180°C/Gas 4. Blanch the spinach in boiling water, then drain it well and squeeze out all the water. Chop the spinach finely and set aside. Put the mixed nuts and cashews in a food processor and pulse until finely chopped, but take care not to reduce them to powder.

Tip the nuts into a large mixing bowl and add the onion, carrot, tinned and sundried tomatoes, egg, cheese, sage, mint, parsley, spinach, garlic, stock and seasoning, then mix everything together well. Grease a loaf tin with butter and pour in the mixture. Cut a piece of greaseproof paper to fit the loaf tin, grease it and lay it over the top to stop the mixture burning. Bake in the preheated oven for about an hour until the nut roast is cooked through. Turn it out onto a plate for slicing.

While the nut roast is cooking, make the mushroom gravy. Gently heat the oil and knob of butter in a medium pan, then add the diced shallot. Sweat for 5 minutes or until transparent. Add the garlic and sweat for 2 minutes. Add the mushrooms and cook gently for a further 5 minutes.

Add the stock and soy sauce, then season to taste and simmer with the lid on the pan for 10 minutes. Mix the tablespoon of flour into the tablespoon of butter and stir into the gravy to thicken it. Serve the gravy piping hot with the nut roast.

ROAST GOOSE
WITH GINGER & ORANGE STUFFING

Roast goose makes a fantastic festive meal and we reckon that you can get six good portions out of one goose. Goose can easily be overcooked, so although it is perfectly possible to stuff the cavity of the bird, it can result in the flesh becoming dry as you wait for the stuffing to cook inside. With this recipe, stuffing balls are cooked separately and then placed around the goose for serving, making a really impressive-looking dish. You can get the stuffing, giblet stock and glaze ready the night before.

SERVES 6

5.5–6kg oven-ready goose
2 medium oranges
6 bay leaves, plus extra for garnish
sea salt flakes
freshly ground black pepper

GINGER & ORANGE STUFFING

1 tbsp sunflower oil
2 medium onions, finely chopped
1 goose liver (if available)
6 balls of stem ginger in syrup, drained
and cut into small pieces
200g fresh white breadcrumbs
500g good-quality sausage meat
3 tbsp finely chopped fresh thyme leaves
sea salt flakes
freshly ground black pepper

GINGER GLAZE

2 balls of stem ginger in syrup, drained
and cut into fine slivers
4 tbsp stem ginger syrup
4 tbsp ginger wine

GINGER WINE GRAVY

2 heaped tbsp plain flour
500ml giblet stock
3 tbsp ginger wine
sea salt flakes
freshly ground black pepper

Remove the goose giblets and the neck from the bird. Make sure the goose is thoroughly thawed if previously frozen. Preheat the oven to 180°C/Gas 4. Place the goose on a rack over a large, sturdy roasting tin and prick with a skewer a few times down each side just below the wing. This will help release the fat. Season the goose with salt and pepper. Finely grate the orange zest and put it in a bowl for later. Cut the oranges into quarters and pop them into the body cavity with the bay leaves and cover the goose legs with triangles of foil. Roast the goose for 30 minutes per kg, plus an extra 20–30 minutes if you like your goose well done. A 6kg goose will need about 3 hours.

While the goose is cooking, prepare the stuffing, glaze and gravy. Separate the liver from the rest of the giblets – it will be the large, softer one. Pat dry on kitchen paper and cut into small pieces, discarding any sinew or damaged parts. Put the rest of the giblets in a big pan with the neck cut into 3 or 4 pieces and make stock in the same way as the turkey stock (see page 108).

To make the stuffing, heat the oil in a large non-stick frying pan and fry the onions for 5 minutes or until softened and lightly browned, stirring occasionally. Add the goose liver and fry for a further 1–2 minutes until browned. Tip into a large bowl and leave to cool. Add the remaining ingredients and the reserved orange zest to the onions and liver. Season with lots of salt and pepper and mix well. Shape the stuffing into 18 small balls and place them on a baking tray, then cover and chill until ready to bake. To make the ginger glaze, put the stem ginger slivers, syrup and ginger wine in a small pan and bring to the boil while stirring. Remove from the heat and set aside until ready to use.

After the goose has been cooking for 1½ hours (or 2 hours if you prefer your goose well done), remove it from the oven and put it on a board. Drain the fat from the roasting tin into a large

heatproof bowl. Return the goose to the rack and continue cooking for a further 1½ hours, removing the foil after 30 minutes.

To check that the goose is cooked, pierce the thickest part of the thigh with a skewer, then press the skewer against the leg and check the juices that run out. When the goose is cooked, the juices should run clear. Also, when you wiggle the legs, they should move fairly freely. Brush the goose with the glaze and put it back in the oven for 5 minutes until the skin is glossy and lightly browned. Don't leave it any longer or the glaze will burn. Take the goose out of the oven and increase the oven temperature to 200°C/Gas 6.

Place the goose on a warmed serving platter and cover loosely with foil and a tea towel and leave to rest for 20–30 minutes. Spoon 3 tablespoons of the reserved goose fat over the stuffing balls to add flavour and bake in the centre of the oven for 20–25 minutes, turning once, until golden brown and cooked throughout.

While the stuffing balls are baking, make the gravy with the giblet stock and ginger wine (see page 109). Remove the tea towel and foil. Place the stuffing balls around the goose, adding a few bay leaves. Pour the gravy into a warmed jug and serve with the goose.

Roast potatoes are fantastic cooked in the goose fat that is released from the bird as it cooks, but creamy mashed potatoes work just as well with goose and are the perfect accompaniment if you only have one oven.

CHRISTMAS TURKEY
WITH TWO STUFFINGS

Some people complain that turkey is dry and tasteless, but it needn't be. We reckon dry turkey is down to overcooking the bird, not the meat itself. Gone are the days of getting up at dawn to put the turkey in – our recipe takes under four hours. Our advice is to watch it carefully towards the end of the cooking time and start testing for doneness around 30 minutes before the calculated time is up. Wrapped in foil and covered with a towel, the turkey will keep warm for up to an hour if necessary.

SERVES 8–10 WITH LEFTOVERS

6kg oven-ready turkey,
thoroughly thawed if frozen
100g softened butter
8 good-quality dry-cured back
or streaky bacon rashers
sea salt flakes
freshly ground black pepper

Put the turkey on a board and remove the neck and giblets, which should be in the body cavity. Make a note of how much the turkey weighs so you can calculate the cooking time. Before you start stuffing the turkey, make sure the inside is completely defrosted. It's important that the heat penetrates right through the bird and into the stuffing so it is thoroughly cooked.

CHESTNUT & SAGE STUFFING

Heat the oil in a frying pan and fry the onion over a low heat until softened and lightly coloured. Add the chopped liver if you saved it when making the giblet stock and fry it with the onion for 2 minutes, while stirring. Tip everything into a large bowl and leave to cool for a while – it's important that the onions are cool before mixing with the uncooked sausage meat. Stir in the rest of the ingredients, mix well with clean hands, then set aside. This stuffing needs to be fairly loose to allow the hot air to circulate around it when it is inside the turkey.

APRICOT & ALMOND STUFFING

Place the same frying pan over a low heat, heat the oil and gently fry the onion and garlic for 5–6 minutes until softened and lightly coloured. Tip everything into a large bowl and leave to cool for a while – it's important that the onions are cool before mixing with the uncooked sausage meat. Stir in the apricots, almonds, sausage meat, zest, breadcrumbs, parsley, salt and pepper. Mix well with clean hands and set aside.

COOKING THE TURKEY

Preheat the oven to 190°C/Gas 5. Use your hands to stuff the chestnut and sage stuffing inside the turkey body cavity. Don't pack it in too tightly as the air needs to circulate around it. Put the apricot and almond stuffing in the neck end of the bird, between the flesh and the skin. Push it in firmly, reaching as far up the breast as you can. Pull the neck flap over the

To make turkey giblet stock, put the giblets, except the liver, in a large pan with the turkey neck, a couple of onions, carrots, celery sticks, bay leaves, some thyme and seasoning. Add a litre of water, bring to the boil and simmer for an hour and a half. Put a lid on the pan for the last 30 minutes so the stock doesn't evaporate too much. Strain through a sieve into a jug and use within 3 days.

CHESTNUT & SAGE STUFFING

1 tbsp sunflower oil
1 medium onion,
turkey liver, finely chopped (optional)
150g vacuum-packed chestnuts,
roughly chopped
225g good-quality pork sausage meat
50g fresh white breadcrumbs
finely grated zest of 1 unwaxed lemon
1 bunch (20–30g) fresh sage, leaves
finely chopped or 1 tbsp dried sage
sea salt flakes
freshly ground black pepper

APRICOT & ALMOND STUFFING

1 tbsp sunflower oil
1 medium onion, finely chopped
1 large garlic clove, crushed
100g no-soak apricots, roughly chopped
100g blanched almonds, toasted and
roughly chopped
225g good-quality pork sausage meat
finely grated zest of 1 well-scrubbed
orange
75g fresh white breadcrumbs
4 tbsp finely chopped fresh parsley
sea salt flakes
freshly ground black pepper

GIBLET GRAVY

2 tbsp plain flour
500ml turkey giblet stock (see opposite)
or reserved vegetable cooking water
100ml red or white wine
sea salt flakes
freshly ground black pepper

Make sure stuffings are thoroughly cooked, with no pinkness in the sausage meat.

stuffing and tuck it under the bird, securing it with a skewer if necessary. Place the turkey, breast side up, in a large, sturdy roasting tin and spread softened butter all over the breast. Season the bird, lay the bacon over the breast and cover the legs with foil. Take a large sheet of foil and wrap it loosely over the whole bird. Either tuck the sides in around the turkey itself or fold them under the edges of the tin to make a tightly sealed parcel. Make sure you leave enough space around the bird for hot air to circulate as it cooks. The legs have a double thickness of foil as they will cook quickly and need some extra protection.

Work out how long the turkey will need to roast by adding 1kg for the stuffings to its weight and calculating 20 minutes cooking time per kg, plus 90 minutes. A 6kg turkey (with stuffing) will need about 3 hours and 50 minutes. Roast the turkey according to your calculations. Roughly 50 minutes before the turkey is due to be ready, remove the foil and continue roasting for 10 minutes or until the bacon crisps and browns. Push the bacon off the breast into the tin and roast for another 10 minutes to brown the breast.

After this time, take the turkey out of the oven and check if it is cooked. The simplest way is to use a meat thermometer inserted into the thickest part of the meat – the temperature should be 71°C. Another way to test the turkey is to pierce the thickest part of the leg with a skewer and press the skewer against the leg. Watch as the juices run out. If they are clear, the turkey is cooked. If they are tinged with pink, the turkey will need to be returned to the oven and cooked for longer. If the turkey is ready, carefully transfer it to a large serving platter – you may need some assistance here. Cover the turkey with foil and place a small towel over it to keep it warm. Leave the turkey to rest for 30 minutes or so while you make the gravy.

MAKING GRAVY

Hold the roasting tin with a dry tea towel at one end, so all the cooking juices run to the corner. Spoon off as much of the turkey fat as possible into a bowl. Try to retain plenty of the cooking juices and sediment as these will add lots of flavour to your gravy. Place the tin on the hob over a medium heat and stir in the flour until thoroughly combined. Slowly add the turkey stock and bring to the boil, stirring constantly. Carefully pour the gravy into a medium saucepan and stir in the wine. Bring to a simmer and cook for 2–3 minutes, stirring regularly. Season to taste with salt and pepper and serve in a warm gravy boat.

CRANBERRY, KUMQUAT & PORT SAUCE

The kumquats in our special version of home-made cranberry sauce give the sauce a really zingy flavour and it's so easy to make.

MAKES A LARGE BOWLFUL

500g fresh cranberries
250g kumquats, sliced thinly
250g caster sugar
6 allspice berries
1 cinnamon stick
3 tbsp port

Bring 250ml of water to boiling point and plunge in the cranberries and the kumquats. Simmer for 10 minutes until they have broken down. Add the sugar, allspice and the cinnamon stick. Stir until the sugar has dissolved and simmer for a further 10 minutes.

Two minutes before the time is up stir in the port. Now the kitchen really smells of Christmas! Discard the allspice and the cinnamon stick and serve the sauce warm or cold.

BRUSSELS SPROUTS & PANCETTA

We guarantee even sprout-haters will love this recipe for lovely caramelised sprouts.

SERVES 10

1kg Brussels sprouts
250g pancetta, cubed
250g roasted chestnuts, peeled and halved
(use the vacuum-packed ones if you wish)
1 dsrstp maple syrup (optional)
sea salt and black pepper

Blanch the sprouts in boiling salted water for 8–10 minutes until tender, then drain and cut them in half. Heat a frying pan over a medium to high heat and fry the pancetta for 5 minutes until crispy and golden. The pancetta will release some fantastic flavoursome fat. Add the drained sprouts, chestnuts and maple syrup to the pancetta pan and mix together. Cook for a further minute or so until the maple syrup begins to caramelise over the sprouts and chestnuts. Remove from the heat and season.

CRISPY ROAST POTATOES

Goose fat is a must to make these the tastiest, crispiest roasties ever.

SERVES 6

2kg good spuds, such as Maris Pipers
100g goose fat
2 tbsp polenta
sea salt flakes
freshly ground black pepper

Preheat the oven to 200–220°C/Gas 6–7. Peel the potatoes and cut them to the size you like. Put them in a pan of water, bring to the boil and cook for about 3 minutes. Drain and shake in a pan to scruff up the surface of the potatoes.

Meanwhile, melt the goose fat in a roasting tin in the hot oven. Sprinkle the polenta over the potatoes and tip the potatoes into the sizzling goose fat. Season liberally with sea salt and black pepper. Cook for about 45 minutes until crispy and golden.

ROAST PARSNIPS

This is a firm favourite with us. Roast the parsnips in honey for a sweet sticky
traditional treat, or try roasting them in maple syrup for a fantastic festive flavour.
Choose your parsnips carefully and remember that they are tastier and sweeter after a frost.

SERVES 6

1kg parsnips
2 tbsp goose fat or vegetable oil
lots of cracked black pepper
sprinkling of sea salt
2 tbsp honey or maple syrup

Preheat the oven to 180°C/Gas 4. Peel and cut the parsnips
into chunks. We tend to cut off the pointy end and then cut
the stouter top into pieces of roughly the same size so they roast
evenly. Heat the goose fat or oil in a roasting tin until smoking.

Toss the parsnip pieces in the hot fat or oil until they are nicely
coated, then sprinkle with the black pepper and sea salt. Place
them in the oven and roast for about 45 minutes or until cooked
and starting to turn golden. The exact cooking time will depend
on how big you cut the chunks, so keep an eye on them.

Add the honey or maple syrup and roll the parsnips in the sticky
juices. Return them to the oven for 10 minutes and continue
cooking until golden. Don't leave them for too long or the honey
or syrup will caramelise too much and turn black and bitter.

GLAZED CARROTS

This is a big favourite at our Christmas dinner. Carrots and
caraway are made for each other – a match made in heaven.

SERVES 6

1kg baby carrots or 8 medium carrots
2 bay leaves
1½ tsp caraway seeds
50g butter
1 dsrtsp runny honey (optional)
a handful of freshly chopped parsley
sea salt flakes
freshly ground black pepper

Wash and peel the carrots. Baby carrots can be left whole but
if using larger ones, cut them into batons of about 5mm thick.
Place the carrots and the bay leaves in a steamer basket and
steam for 5–7 minutes until softened, or boil them for the same
amount of time.

Meanwhile, put the caraway seeds in a dry pan and fry
them for about a minute over a low to medium heat. Remove
from the heat and allow to cool. Place the seeds in a pestle and
mortar and grind them to make a rough powder. Melt the butter
and honey, if using, in a pan and add the ground caraway seeds
and carrots. Toss the carrots in the honey and caraway butter,
add seasoning to taste and cook for a couple of minutes over
a medium heat. Mix in the freshly chopped parsley and serve.

BROAD BEANS
WITH PANCETTA & SHALLOTS

SERVES 4–6

400g frozen broad beans, defrosted
4 tbsp olive oil
150g pancetta, finely diced
4 shallots, finely chopped

Defrost the beans and remove the tough outer skins. This is a bit of a job but well worth the effort, believe us, and defrosted beans are easier to peel than fresh ones. Warm the olive oil and sauté the pancetta and the shallots until the shallots are soft and the pancetta golden. Add the beans and simmer for a further 2 minutes. Season and serve.

MASH

The diversity of the humble potato is best illustrated when you MASH it! Mash creates a blank canvas for you to create your culinary fancy by adding some key ingredients to lift it out of the ordinary to take a major supporting role for any dinner. We're going to give you some ideas to get your culinary juices going, then it's up to you. Experiment and have fun.

There's nothing worse than lumpy mash. Make sure your spuds are all cut into the same size so they'll cook evenly.

Buy floury spuds. Desiree, King Edwards and Maris Pipers are all good options.

Always heat the cream and melt the butter so your mash stays warm. Make the effort to mash your spuds well, it's really worth it. Think of it as low-impact aerobics.

Use white pepper. It makes the mash more potatoey.

MUSTARD MASH
Prepare your mash – poaching the potatoes in simmering water rather than boiling gives best results. Then add 2 teaspoons of Dijon mustard and a dessertspoon of wholegrain mustard to every 1kg of potatoes.

SAGE & ONION MASH
This is fab with poultry and game. Blanch the sage leaves in hot water for a minute or so – this helps take the bitterness out of the leaves. Chop the leaves finely and set aside. Boil the onions until tender, but not soft, and drain well. Chop the cooked onions, add the sage and mix well. Add the sage and onion mix to your mash and stir through. Season to taste.

ROAST GARLIC MASH
Place a bulb of garlic on a large square of foil, drizzle it with oil and wrap it up. Bake the garlic at 190°C/Gas 5 until soft, about 30 minutes, then cool. Melt some butter, then separate the cloves and pop the flesh out of the skins into the melted butter. Leave to infuse for a good 5 minutes over a low heat. Remove the garlic from the butter and stir the garlicky butter through the mash. Add half a teaspoon of truffle oil too, if you like.

BLACK PUDDING MASH
This mash is great with roast pork, chops or bangers. Remove the skin and dice the black pudding into small pieces. Fry these and then stir through your mash. Heaven!

CHIPOLATAS WRAPPED IN BACON & DATES WRAPPED IN BACON

Chipolatas in bacon have to be everybody's favourite garnish. It's best to make your own – you'll find that they're miles away from the liquid pig constructions that you buy from the freezer cabinet. Mix in some dates wrapped in bacon to give you a lovely sticky sweet and sour vibe.

SERVES 8

500g thin-cut streaky bacon rashers
500g good-quality chipolata sausages
1 box of dried or Medjool dates, pitted

Preheat the oven to 180°C/Gas 4. Stretch the bacon rashers by firmly drawing the back of a large carving knife along each rasher so it becomes longer and thinner. This will make the bacon crispier. Cut the rashers in half lengthwise. Wrap a piece of bacon around each sausage and a piece around each date. Continue until all the ingredients are used up. Place these little bundles on a greased baking sheet with the join of the rasher on the underside in each case.

Cook in the preheated oven for about 20 minutes until the bacon is crispy and the sausage is cooked through. Scatter like pig confetti around the turkey!

BREAD SAUCE

The bread sauce sits alongside the giblet gravy and the cranberry sauce to garnish your Christmas dinner. We love pieces of moist warm turkey dipped in this most traditional of sauces. This is another one of those jobs that you can partly get out of the way on Christmas Eve.

SERVES 8

1 litre whole milk
1 onion, quartered
8 cloves
2 bay leaves
white breadcrumbs made from 1 small day-old loaf, crusts removed
large knob of unsalted butter
2 tbsp double cream
freshly grated nutmeg to taste
white pepper and sea salt to taste

Pour the milk into a pan and bring it to a simmer. Meanwhile, stud each onion quarter with 2 cloves. We like it like this, but if you want a less clovey flavour to your sauce, reduce the number of cloves. Place the onion quarters into the pan with the bay leaves and simmer gently for about 3 minutes. Leave this to infuse, preferably overnight, and you will have lovely spiced milk.

When you are ready to make the sauce, strain the milk and discard the onions, cloves and bay leaves. Warm the milk in a pan, add the breadcrumbs and simmer until the crumbs have expanded and the sauce has thickened. If it seems too thick add some more milk or if it's too thin, add extra breadcrumbs. Stir in the butter and the cream, season to taste and serve warm, finished off with a liberal sprinkling of freshly grated nutmeg. We like this with lots of white pepper. Yo ho ho!

CLASSIC BRANDY BUTTER

Perfect with Christmas pud or mince pies.

SERVES 6–8

175g unsalted butter, at room
temperature
225g icing sugar
4–6 tbsp brandy

Put the butter in a food processor with the icing sugar and blend until smooth and pale. You may need to remove the lid and push the mixture down a couple of times. With the motor running, slowly pour in the brandy and blitz until smooth. Taste every so often and adjust the amount of brandy accordingly. Pile it into a serving dish, cover with clingfilm and chill. Use within 5–6 days as the butter can start to taste slightly stale the longer it is exposed to air.

BRANDY SAUCE

Brandy sauce can be a rather insipid white sauce flavoured with throat-chokingly harsh brandy – and the packet mixes are even worse. Our brandy sauce is enriched with eggs, rather like proper custard, and will do your Christmas pudding proud. Use rum instead of brandy if you prefer – try Jamaican spiced rum for a change.

MAKES A BIG JUGFUL

2 large free-range egg yolks
1–2 tbsp brandy or dark rum
2 heaped tsp cornflour
25g caster sugar
250ml whole milk
250ml double cream

Put the egg yolks with the brandy or rum in a medium saucepan and add the cornflour and sugar. Whisk until smooth. Gradually whisk in the milk and cream. Put the pan over a low heat and cook gently for 6–8 minutes, whisking constantly, until the sauce is smooth and thick. Taste and add a little more alcohol if you fancy and serve immediately.

BRANDY CREAM

This is really rich and luxurious – go on, spoil yourself.

MAKES A BIG BOWLFUL

300ml fresh double cream, well chilled
2 tbsp caster sugar
2 tbsp brandy or Cointreau
(orange liqueur)
finely grated zest of ½ orange (optional)

Pour the cream into a large bowl and stir in the sugar, brandy or Cointreau and orange zest, if using. Using an electric whisk, whip the cream until it forms soft peaks. Transfer to a pretty bowl and serve in generous dollops. If you want to make this a few hours in advance, cover the bowl with clingfilm and chill until ready to serve. You might need to give the cream another quick whisk before serving.

CHRISTMAS PANNA COTTA

Not everyone likes traditional Christmas pud so here's a delicious alternative –
a spicy panna cotta. It's light, modern and sexy – just like us really!

SERVES 6

2 tbsp raisins
2 tbsp dark rum
3½ sheets of gelatine
500ml double cream
4 tbsp caster sugar
¼ tsp ground ginger
¼ tsp ground allspice
¼ tsp ground nutmeg
¼ tsp ground cinnamon
1 small handful of berries, such
as redcurrants, to serve

Put the raisins in a bowl, add the rum and leave them to soak for about 30 minutes. Soak the gelatine in cold water until soft.

Meanwhile, pour the cream into a heavy saucepan, add the sugar and spices and bring to the boil. Then reduce the heat and simmer the cream for 2–3 minutes. Take the pan off the heat, squeeze the excess water out of the gelatine and whisk it into the cream mixture. Drain the raisins and add them to the cream, discarding the rum.

Divide the mixture between 6 moulds or ramekins. Set them aside to cool completely, then cover the panna cottas with clingfilm and chill in the fridge for at least 2 hours, or until set.

When you're ready to serve the panna cottas, dip the moulds into hot water for a minute to loosen them and turn them out onto plates. Serve with some berries – redcurrants look very Christmassy!

Rum-soaked raisins add a lovely seasonal touch to this classic.

CRANBERRY, DATE & MACADAMIA PUDDING
WITH BUTTERSCOTCH SAUCE

You're going to love our funky Christmas pud – it's much lighter than a traditional pudding and filled with plump cranberries, soft dates and crunchy macadamia nuts. It needs to be made on the day itself, but you can get all the dry ingredients ready the day before.

SERVES 6–8

butter, for greasing the bowl
3 tbsp orange liqueur, such as Cointreau
100g dried cranberries
175g butter, at room temperature
150g soft light brown sugar
finely grated zest of 1 orange
2 tsp ground mixed spice
3 large free-range eggs, beaten
200g self-raising flour
100g macadamia or pecan nuts, roughly chopped
150g dates, roughly chopped

BUTTERSCOTCH SAUCE
200g soft light brown sugar
50g butter, cut into cubes
4 tbsp golden syrup
200ml double cream
4 tbsp orange liqueur, such as Cointreau

If you want to make individual puds instead of a big one, just steam for 40 minutes.

Generously butter a 1.5-litre pudding basin, line the base with a circle of baking parchment and set aside. Pour the orange liqueur for the pudding into a small pan and add the cranberries. Bring to the boil and cook for 1–2 minutes, stirring constantly, or until all the liquid has evaporated. Tip into a bowl and leave to cool.

Put the 175g of butter into a large bowl and add the sugar, zest and spice. Beat with an electric whisk for about 5 minutes or until light and fluffy. Whisk half the eggs into the creamed mixture, then whisk in half the flour. Whisk in the remaining eggs and finally the rest of the flour. Add the nuts, then stir in the dates and cranberries. Spoon into the basin and smooth the surface.

Cover the bowl with a large circle of baking parchment, with a pleat in the middle to allow for expansion. Cover the parchment with foil, again with a pleat. Tie both tightly in place with string. Make a handle across the basin with any excess string.

Place the pud on an upturned saucer or trivet in a large saucepan and add enough just-boiled water to come halfway up the sides of the basin. Cover the pan with a tight-fitting lid and steam in simmering water for 2 hours, adding more water if necessary. When the pudding is done, carefully lift the basin from the water and leave the pudding to stand for 5–10 minutes before serving.

Meanwhile, make the butterscotch sauce. Put the sugar, butter, syrup and cream in a saucepan and stir over a low heat until the sugar dissolves. Simmer gently for 1–2 minutes until the sauce is smooth. Gradually add the liqueur and let the sauce bubble for about a minute, stirring constantly. Remove from the heat.

Remove the foil and paper from the pud. Loosen the sides of the pudding with a knife and turn it out onto a deep plate. Remove the paper and pour over some sauce. Serve the pudding in wedges with more sauce and lots of double cream or ice cream.

Boxing
Day

TURKEY & VEGETABLE SOUP

This soup is a great antidote to all the rich Christmas food. A full-flavoured turkey stock makes a light and delicious base to which diced turkey, vegetables and pasta are added. You can add any vegetables you have around – just remember to cut them up fairly small so they cook in about the same time. If you don't have any pasta handy, use a couple of diced potatoes instead. If possible, prepare the stock the day before you make the soup so it can set to a soft jelly and you can remove the fat.

SERVES 6

1 cooked turkey carcass
5 medium carrots, scrubbed
4 celery sticks, trimmed
2 onions, peeled and cut into wedges
2 bay leaves
1 small bunch of fresh thyme
12 peppercorns
75g vermicelli pasta or spaghetti,
broken into short lengths
2 slender leeks, trimmed
2 tbsp finely chopped fresh parsley (optional)
sea salt flakes
freshly ground black pepper

Put the carcass on a chopping board and strip away and discard the skin. Take off as much meat as possible from the carcass – you will need about 250g for the soup. Cut the carcass into 3 or 4 pieces with a heavy knife and put them into the largest pan you have. Cut 2 of the carrots into big chunks and 2 of the celery sticks into short lengths. Add these to the pan with the onions, herbs and peppercorns.

Pour about 2.5 litres of water into the pan. The water should just cover the bones and vegetables. Cover the pan loosely with a lid and place over a medium heat. Bring to the boil, then reduce the heat immediately and leave to simmer gently for 1½ hours – it's important the stock doesn't boil furiously or it will become cloudy. As the liquid reduces, you may need to turn the turkey bones every now and then. You want about 1.5 litres of stock for the soup, so if the liquid appears to be reducing too much, add a little more water to the pan.

At the end of the cooking time, tip the turkey bones, vegetables and stock into a colander placed over a large bowl to collect all the liquid. Cool, then cover the liquid and chill overnight. The stock should set to a soft jelly as it cools. Throw away the bones and veg. Next day, scrape away and discard any fat that has risen to the surface of the liquid and tip the jellied stock into a saucepan. Peel and dice the remaining carrots and finely slice the celery. Add the vegetables to the pan with the stock.

Bring to the boil, add the vermicelli or spaghetti and cook for 10 minutes or until the carrots and pasta are tender, stirring occasionally. Finely slice the leeks and rinse them well. Add the turkey meat and leeks to the pan for the last 5 minutes of the cooking time. Season with salt and pepper to taste and stir in the chopped parsley if using. Ladle the soup into warmed bowls and serve.

If you don't have time to chill the stock overnight, leave it to settle in a jug for 20 minutes or so and then spoon off as much fat as you can.

COLD TURKEY & HAM PIE
WITH CRANBERRY TOPPING

This is a fantastic, well-packed pie that's best eaten cold with some salad and crisps.
We use a 23cm springform cake tin when we're making this and it works really well.

SERVES 4–6

PASTRY
450g plain flour
2 tsp baking powder
1 tsp salt
60g cold butter, cut into cubes
60g cold lard, cut into cubes

CRANBERRY TOPPING
500g fresh cranberries
250g kumquats, sliced thinly
250g caster sugar
6 allspice berries
1 cinnamon stick
3 tbsp port
2 gelatine leaves

FILLING
1 tbsp olive oil
1 tbsp butter
1 onion, chopped
1 leek, chopped
2 small celery sticks, chopped
1 dsrtsp flour
100ml chicken or turkey stock
3 tbsp double cream
½ tsp English mustard powder
a good handful of curly parsley, chopped
350g cooked ham, cut into chunks
500g cooked turkey, dark and light meat, in large pieces
sea salt flakes
freshly ground black pepper

First make the pastry. Put the flour in a food processor with the baking powder and salt. Add the butter and lard and blitz to crumbs. Add about 140ml of water, a little at a time, and process until a ball of pastry forms. Wrap the pastry in clingfilm and leave it to chill in the fridge.

Next make the cranberry topping. Bring 150ml of water to the boil. Add the cranberries and kumquats and simmer them for 10 minutes until they have broken down. Add the sugar, allspice and the cinnamon stick. Stir until the sugar has dissolved and simmer for a further 10 minutes. Add the port and bring back to the boil for a couple of minutes, then remove the pan from the heat. Place the gelatine in a bowl of cold water for about 3 minutes to swell and soften. Drain and stir the softened gelatine into the cranberry sauce. Leave to cool, then place in the fridge to set.

Next bake the pastry blind. Preheat the oven to 170°C/Gas 3. Line a 23cm springform cake tin with silicone baking paper. Roll the pastry out and line the tin, leaving the pastry hanging over the edge for trimming later. Cover the pastry with a piece of baking parchment and fill with baking beans. Bake in the preheated oven for 15–20 minutes until cooked, then remove the beans and paper and trim the pastry neatly. Set the pastry case aside to cool.

Now make the filling. Put the oil and butter in a large frying pan, add the onion, leek and celery and sweat for about 5 minutes. Stir in the flour, then add the stock and cook until thickened. Add the cream, mustard powder and parsley, then fold in the ham and turkey. Season to taste – use lots of pepper but go carefully with the salt, as your ham may be salty. Pack the filling into the pastry case and put the pie in the oven for 15 minutes at 170°C/Gas 3 for the flavours to bake together. Remove and leave to cool for a while, then spread on the cranberry topping. The heat from the pie will melt the jelly slightly, which helps it settle into the pie. Leave the pie to cool completely and serve cold.

GOOSE RISOTTO

If you have any leftover goose from your Christmas dinner, this risotto is an excellent way of using it up. It's great made with turkey too. The green peppercorns add a lovely spicy freshness.

SERVES 4

3 tbsp olive oil
4 shallots, peeled and finely chopped
2 garlic cloves, crushed
1 litre chicken stock
400g risotto rice (arborio or carnaroli)
1 tbsp whole green peppercorns
2 tbsp butter
250g chestnut mushrooms, finely sliced
500g leftover goose meat, finely chopped
1 tbsp chopped mixed fresh herbs
(sage, rosemary, parsley, tarragon, chives)
4 tbsp freshly grated Parmesan
sea salt flakes
freshly ground black pepper

Heat 2 tablespoons of the oil in a large, heavy-bottomed saucepan and fry the shallots until they have softened but not browned. Add the garlic and continue to cook for another couple of minutes. Meanwhile, pour the stock into another pan and bring it to simmering point.

Add the rice to the shallots and sauté and stir for a couple of minutes. Start adding a ladle or two of hot stock and then add the peppercorns. As each ladleful of stock is absorbed, add more and keep adding the hot stock and stirring the risotto until the rice is cooked but still al dente. This should take about 20 minutes.

Heat the rest of the oil in a frying pan and add a tablespoon of the butter. Add the mushrooms and sauté until cooked.

Fold the mushrooms and goose meat into the cooked rice, then add the rest of the butter, the herbs and the Parmesan. Season to taste and serve.

WARM PIGEON BREAST SALAD
WITH LIME MARMALADE DRESSING

This makes a great starter or light main course. The lime marmalade adds a wonderful tanginess that's perfect with the pigeon and is also good with duck breast.

SERVES 4–6

125g dry-cured, smoked bacon rashers, rinds removed
2 tbsp olive oil
4 pigeon breasts
100g black pudding, diced
salad leaves, such as rocket, watercress and spinach, for serving
280g Anya (or similar) potatoes, boiled, cooled and sliced

LIME MARMALADE DRESSING
2 heaped tbsp Rose's lemon and lime marmalade
juice of ½ orange
1 tbsp balsamic vinegar
2 tbsp olive oil

First make the dressing. Melt the marmalade in a small pan over a low heat, then add the orange juice, vinegar and oil. Heat until warm, stirring all the time. Remove the pan from the heat and keep the dressing warm.

Cut the bacon rashers into diagonal slices. Heat the olive oil in a frying pan over a medium heat and fry the bacon for 2 minutes until brown. Add the pigeon breasts and cook for a further 2 minutes until coloured. Add the black pudding and warm through for another minute. Remove the pan from the heat and leave to rest for a moment or two.

Arrange some salad leaves on each plate and cover with a layer of sliced potatoes. Add the bacon, slices of pigeon breast and black pudding on top, then drizzle over the warm dressing. Serve with some crusty bread to mop up the juices.

TURKEY CURRY

This simple curry is made mainly from store cupboard ingredients, but it has a lovely fresh taste and mouth-watering aroma. You don't have to add the tomatoes and spinach leaves, but they do give extra colour and flavour. Use new potatoes if you like a fairly thin sauce, but if you prefer it thicker, use Maris Pipers or similar. The starch in the spuds will thicken the sauce as it cooks. You can serve the curry with rice if you like, but it's just as good without. This recipe makes a medium curry, so if you like your curry hot, add a little more chilli powder or fry a finely chopped chilli with the garlic.

SERVES 6

600g new or old potatoes
2 tbsp sunflower oil
2 medium onions, halved and sliced
2 garlic cloves, finely sliced
2 tsp ground coriander
2 tsp ground cumin
½ tsp ground turmeric
½ tsp ground ginger
½ tsp hot chilli powder or cayenne pepper
1 tbsp tomato purée
1 litre chicken or turkey stock, fresh
or made with 1 chicken stock cube
3 tbsp mango chutney
2 bay leaves
500g cooked turkey, breast or leg meat,
cut into chunky pieces
4 tomatoes, quartered
200g young spinach leaves
sea salt flakes
freshly ground black pepper

If using new potatoes, simply scrub and halve them. If using big old potatoes, peel them and cut into thick slices.

Heat the oil in a large, non-stick saucepan and cook the onions for 5 minutes over a low heat until softened and lightly coloured. Add the garlic and cook for 1 minute more. Sprinkle all the spices over the onions and cook for 1–2 minutes, stirring constantly. Stir in the tomato purée and fry with the onions and spices for a few seconds before pouring in the stock. Add the potatoes, mango chutney and bay leaves and season well with salt and pepper. Bring to the boil, then reduce the heat slightly and simmer for 10 minutes, stirring occasionally.

Add the leftover turkey to the curry and return to a gentle simmer. Cook for 10 minutes, stirring once or twice. Next, add the tomatoes and scatter over the spinach leaves. Cover the pan with a lid and simmer gently for a further 5 minutes or until the tomatoes are soft and the spinach has wilted. Stir through the curry gently. Serve with spiced basmati rice if you like and yoghurt.

TURKEY SANDWICH
WITH CHIPS & GRAVY

More of a suggestion than a recipe, we know, but one of our favourite Boxing Day treats. Chips and gravy might sound a bit common, but they're heaven with the soggy gravy-infused sarnie.

SERVES 4

cold turkey
8 slices of ordinary white bread
butter
leftover gravy

CHIPS
4 large potatoes, preferably Maris Pipers or Yukon Gold (you want a potato that has more fibre than water)
2 litres sunflower oil
sea salt flakes
malt vinegar

Peel the potatoes and cut them lengthways into slices of about 1cm thick. Cut each slice into fairly thick chips and rinse them in a colander under plenty of cold water to remove excess starch. If you have time, it's worth letting the chips soak in a bowl of cold water for several hours or overnight. Blot them dry on kitchen paper.

Heat the oil to 130°C. Gently drop half the chips into the hot oil and leave them to fry for 10 minutes or so, until cooked through but not browned. Remove them from the pan and drain on plenty of kitchen paper. Follow the same method with the rest of the chips and drain well. The chips can be left for several hours at this stage.

Make your turkey sandwiches – we don't need to tell you how to do that – and warm the gravy through gently.

When ready to serve, reheat the oil to 190°C. Lower all the chips gently into the pan and cook them for 4–5 minutes until crisp and golden brown. Lift them out and drain on kitchen paper. Serve onto the plates and sprinkle with salt and vinegar. Add your sandwiches to one side and drizzle on the hot gravy. Great with pickled onions too.

The secret of really good chips is to cook them twice at different temperatures. It's best to use a deep-fat fryer if you have one.

TURKEY & HAM PANCAKES

This is a great way of making a small amount of leftover turkey and ham into a filling meal. If you don't have leftovers, buy the meat from the deli counter. You can get everything ready in advance if you like, then warm the pancakes in a microwave while you reheat the filling. Lovely with a green salad.

SERVES 4 (MAKES 8 PANCAKES)

65g butter
½ medium onion, finely chopped
50g plain flour
500ml semi-skimmed milk
200g good-quality ham
200g leftover roast turkey, skinned
75ml white wine or chicken stock
1 heaped tbsp finely chopped fresh parsley
or 1 tsp freeze-dried parsley
a good pinch of freeze-dried tarragon
1 bay leaf
a good grating of whole nutmeg
1 tbsp sunflower oil
100g baby button mushrooms, wiped and
halved or sliced if large
sea salt flakes
freshly ground black pepper

PANCAKES
115g plain flour
2 large eggs
300ml semi-skimmed milk
15g butter
1 tbsp oil

Start with the filling for the pancakes. Melt 50g of the butter in a non-stick pan and gently fry the onion until softened, stirring regularly. Sprinkle over the flour and stir it into the onion. Cook for a few seconds, then gradually add the milk, stirring well between each addition. Bring the sauce to a gentle simmer and cook for 2–3 minutes, stirring constantly. Cut the ham and turkey into small pieces and stir them into the sauce. Add the wine or stock and the herbs. Season with nutmeg, salt and pepper and cook over a low heat for 5 minutes, stirring regularly.

Meanwhile, melt the remaining butter and the oil in a small frying pan and stir fry the mushrooms over a high heat for 2–3 minutes until golden. Stir them into the turkey and ham mixture, check the seasoning and add a little more wine or stock if necessary. The mixture should be thick and creamy. Cover the surface with clingfilm to prevent a skin forming and set aside.

To make the pancakes, blitz the flour, eggs and milk in a food processor until smooth and pour the batter into a jug. Melt the butter and oil in a small pan, then remove from the heat. Put a small non-stick frying pan over a medium-high heat and brush with some of the melted fat. Pour a little of the batter into the pan and swirl around until the base of the pan is completely covered. Cook for 1–2 minutes or until the bottom of the pancake is golden. Loosen the sides with a palette knife, flip over and cook the other side for 40–60 seconds. Put the pancake on a plate and make the rest of the pancakes in the same way. Pile up the pancakes on the plate, placing squares of baking parchment between each layer, and keep warm in a low oven.

When you're ready to eat, warm the filling over a low heat until it's piping hot, stirring regularly. You may need to add a splash of milk to get it to the right consistency. Spoon roughly an eighth of the mixture onto one side of a warm pancake and fold it over. Repeat with the remaining pancakes and filling.

BRANDY SNAPS
WITH GINGER CREAM & CHOCOLATE

Enjoy these on Boxing Day afternoon with a nice cup of tea. The stem ginger in
the cream adds a touch of luxury and the drizzly dark chocolate on top reminds
us of chocolate gingers – another Christmas favourite.

MAKES 16

75g butter, plus extra for greasing
75g caster sugar
3 tbsp golden syrup
75g plain flour
1 tsp ground ginger
2 tsp brandy
finely grated zest of ½ large lemon

FILLING
300ml double cream
4 balls of stem ginger in syrup, drained
and finely chopped
100g plain dark chocolate, broken into
squares

Put the cooked brandy snaps in an airtight container with pieces of baking parchment between them and they should last for 24 hours before becoming soft. Only fill them up to 1 hour before serving.

Preheat the oven to 180°C/Gas 4. Melt the butter with the sugar and syrup, stirring over a low heat until the sugar dissolves. Remove the pan from the heat and stir in the flour, ginger, brandy and lemon zest.

Line 2 flat baking trays with baking parchment. Place 4 scant tablespoons of the brandy snap mixture on one of the baking sheets, leaving plenty of room between them to allow for spreading. Bake in the centre of the oven for 10–12 minutes or until bubbly and deep golden brown. Meanwhile, place 4 more scant tablespoons of the brandy snap mixture on the second baking tray. Grease the handles of 2 wooden spoons with butter and wrap a rubber band around them to bind them together.

Take the first batch of brandy snaps out of the oven and put the second tray in to bake for the same amount of time. Let the brandy snaps rest for 30–60 seconds, then lift one off with a palette knife and wrap it carefully around the handles of the spoons, overlapping a little. Hold for around 30 seconds until the biscuit sets in a tube shape, then gently slide it off and put it on a rack to cool. Repeat with the remaining brandy snaps. If the biscuits become too hard to roll, simply return them to the oven for a few seconds to soften. Continue baking and rolling the brandy snaps until all the mixture is used.

To prepare the filling, whip the cream until soft peaks form. Stir in the chopped ginger and spoon into a large piping bag fitted with a plain nozzle. Pipe the ginger cream into each end of the brandy snaps and place them on a rack placed over a board.

One hour before serving, melt the chocolate in a heatproof bowl over a pan of simmering water. Remove from the heat and, drizzle melted chocolate over the brandy snaps. Leave in a cool place for 30–60 minutes or until the chocolate sets. Carefully put them onto a serving plate and enjoy yourselves!

The perfect cheeseboard

A good cheeseboard to round off your dinner is a real Christmas treat. We spoke to cheesemonger Michael Jones about how to choose cheese and treat it right.

A cheeseboard doesn't have to be expensive. If you're putting together a selection for a big gathering you might like to choose half a dozen or more cheeses, but it can also be nice to buy just one or two really good cheeses to enjoy.

With a larger cheeseboard, it's a good idea to include different milk varieties – look for a goat's milk cheese and one made from sheep's milk as well as cow's milk cheeses. Choose different textures too – a firm hard cheese, a blue, and something with a soft creamy texture. Try to balance the flavours and textures, but there are no hard and fast rules. You might like to choose cheeses from just one area, as we have done here with British and Irish cheeses, or serve cheese from a particular region of a country with local wines to match.

If you can, buy cheese freshly cut from a specialist shop, a cheese counter or perhaps from a farmers' market. That way you'll get the best, freshest flavours. A whole cheese is a living, maturing thing and once it's cut into, it stops ripening and developing. If you buy cheese that's been cut, wrapped and left to sit on a shelf for weeks you're really not getting the best. Look for cheese in the peak of condition, ready to serve. Once you get it home, store it in the fridge loosely wrapped in waxed paper. Keep it well away from any contaminants, such as raw meat.

Most important is to take your cheese out of the fridge a couple of hours before serving so it can come up to room temperature and you'll be able to taste it properly. If the cheese is too cold, you won't get the full flavour. If you have a big piece of cheese, cut off what you need for serving and leave the rest in the fridge – it doesn't do cheese any good to be warmed up and cooled down too often.

Serve the cheese with some bread if you like or, better still after a big meal, some savoury biscuits or crackers. You might like to serve some chutney, such as our Christmas chutney (see page 29), or a fruit jelly, such as the Spanish membrillo, which is made of quince and goes a treat with Manchego, a Spanish sheep's milk cheese. Pears with an Italian cheese called Pecorino are another great combo.

Cornish Yarg

Keen's Farm Cheddar

Appleby's
Red Cheshire

Swaledale
(sheep's milk)

Colston Bassett
Stilton

Ardrahan

Caerphilly

Barkham
Blue

Devon goat
cheese with
herbs and garlic

Smoked Wedmore

Breakfasts & brunches

CINNAMON SWIRLS

The smell of warm cinnamon and sugar when these are baking is almost more
than flesh and blood can stand. Try them – you won't be disappointed.

MAKES 16

375ml milk
100g butter, cut into pieces
75g soft light brown sugar
650g strong plain flour, plus
extra for dusting
a good pinch of salt
7g sachet of fast-action dried yeast
1 medium free-range egg, beaten

FILLING
100g butter
100g soft light brown sugar
25g ground almonds
2 tbsp ground cinnamon

TOPPING
25g butter
½ tsp ground cinnamon
2 tsp caster sugar

You will need 2 baking trays lined with baking parchment.
Pour the milk into a pan, add the butter and sugar. Place
over a medium heat until the butter is melted and the
mixture is warm, but don't let it get too hot. Remove from
the heat and set aside.

Put the flour in a large bowl and stir in the salt and yeast. Stir
the beaten egg into the warm milk and pour it onto the flour
mixture. Mix with a wooden spoon and then with your clean
hands until the mixture forms a soft, spongy dough.

Turn out onto a well-floured surface and knead for 10 minutes.
The dough will be fairly wet to begin with, but within a few
minutes it should feel less sticky. You can always sprinkle a
little extra flour over the surface while kneading if necessary.
Set aside while you make the filling.

For the filling, cream the butter in a bowl with the brown
sugar, ground almonds and cinnamon. Roll out the dough on
a well-floured surface to form a rectangle of about 35 x 50cm.
Using a rubber spatula or palette knife, spread the filling over
the dough, taking it all the way to the edges.

Roll the dough up from one of the longest sides, keeping it
fairly tight. Trim the ends and cut the dough into 2cm rounds.
Brush the pastry with a little water if it begins to undo. Place
the rounds on the baking trays, leaving plenty of room between
them. Leave to rise in a warm place for 45–60 minutes or until
doubled in size.

Preheat the oven to 220°C/Gas 7. For the topping, melt the
butter in a small pan and brush it over the cinnamon swirls.
Mix the cinnamon and caster sugar and sprinkle this over the
buns. Bake the swirls for 10–12 minutes or until well risen
and pale golden brown. Cool on the tins for a few minutes
before serving.

Leftover buns can be stored in a large airtight tin for 2-3 days. Warm through in a hot oven before serving.

SMOKED SALMON,
DILL & RICOTTA FRITTERS
WITH LIME-SEARED SCALLOPS

This decadent brunch brings a lovely hint of summer to brighten the dark days after Christmas.
A dish that we always say is lighter and fresher than a Christmas fairy!

SERVES 4

250g ricotta
2 tbsp plain flour
½ tsp sea salt flakes
½ tsp freshly ground black pepper
1 free-range egg, beaten
100g smoked salmon, finely chopped
1 sprig of dill, finely chopped
grated zest of ½ lemon
1 tsp lemon juice
olive oil, for frying
4 king scallops
squeeze of lime

GARNISH
1 bunch of watercress
1 bunch of basil
4 plum tomatoes, sliced
olive oil
balsamic vinegar

Mix the ricotta, flour, sea salt, black pepper, egg, smoked salmon, dill and lemon zest and juice together in a bowl. Set aside to chill if you have time.

Heat a tablespoon of olive oil in a large frying pan and when it's hot add a tablespoon of the fritter mixture. Cook until the mixture starts to go golden, then carefully turn it over with a palette knife and continue cooking until firm and golden on both sides. Put the fritter on a plate and keep warm in a low oven while you make the rest of the fritters in the same way. Add more oil to the pan as needed.

Meanwhile, divide the watercress between 4 plates, add some torn basil leaves and sliced tomatoes. Dress with olive oil and a little balsamic vinegar.

When the fritters are ready, heat some oil in another pan and when it's very hot add the scallops, season and give them a squirt of lime. The hot scallops will draw in the lime. Place 1 or 2 fritters, depending on their size, onto each plate of salad and top with a seared scallop.

CORNED BEEF HASH & POACHED EGGS
WITH JUMBO PRETZELS

There's nothing better for brunch than proper corned beef hash with perfectly poached eggs, the yellow yolk oozing over the hash. Serve with some jumbo pretzels if you like.

SERVES 4

CORNED BEEF HASH
50g unsalted butter
1 onion, peeled and chopped
700g or so floury potatoes, cooked and diced
1 x 340g tin of corned beef, cubed
1 tbsp Worcestershire sauce
1 tbsp chopped fresh parsley
sea salt flakes
freshly ground black pepper

POACHED EGGS
4 fresh free-range eggs
white wine vinegar

JUMBO PRETZELS
1 sachet of fast-action dried yeast
1kg strong white bread flour
4 tsp sea salt
1 tsp caster sugar
1 tbsp olive oil
1 free-range egg, beaten
poppy seeds
sea salt flakes

To make the corned beef hash, melt the butter in a heavy frying pan and sweat the onion until golden. Add the potatoes and the corned beef, stir and cook until crisp. Burnt bits are good so let the bottom catch in places. When the hash is ready, mix in the Worcestershire sauce and parsley and season.

We're going to tell you how to make perfect poached eggs. First you have to have fresh eggs, really fresh. Use a large, high-sided frying pan. Fill it two-thirds full of water and bring the water to the boil. Now here's our secret – place the eggs, still in their shells, into the boiling water for precisely 20 seconds. Remove and turn the heat down so the water is simmering. Add a glug of white wine vinegar to the pan, swirl lightly and crack the eggs into the water. The eggs will retain their shape beautifully. Poach for about 3 minutes depending on how you like your eggs. Serve on the hash.

JUMBO PRETZELS
First make the starter sponge. Pour about 680ml of warm water into a large bowl and whisk in the yeast until dissolved. Stir in 500g of the flour – the mixture will be sloppy at this stage. Cover with clingfilm or a damp tea towel and leave in a warm place for a couple of hours until the sponge has increased in size and there are lots of bubbles.

Put the rest of the flour in a large bowl and stir in the salt and sugar. Add the olive oil and the starter sponge, then work everything together. If the dough seems too heavy, add a little more water; if too sloppy, add more flour. Turn the dough out onto a floured surface. Roll it out into a rope shape about 2cm thick and shape 4–6 massive pretzels. Place on a greased baking tray, cover and leave to rise in a warm place for 30 minutes or so. Preheat the oven to 220°C/Gas 7.

Mix the egg with a tablespoon of water and brush over the pretzels. Sprinkle with poppy seeds and salt flakes, then bake in the oven for 30 minutes until cooked through and golden.

AMERICAN BANANA PANCAKES
WITH STREAKY BACON

The idea for this came from a bacon and banana sandwich we had in South Africa. Morph the bacon and banana into an American pancake stack and you have a real Christmas treat.

SERVES 4 (MAKES 12 PANCAKES)

50g butter, cubed
275g self-raising flour
1 tsp baking powder
2 large free-range eggs
2 tbsp soft light brown sugar
300ml whole milk
1 large banana, roughly chopped
1–2 tbsp sunflower oil
8 streaky bacon rashers, rinds removed
maple syrup

Preheat the oven to 120°C/Gas ½. Melt 25g of the butter in a small pan over a low heat and leave to cool for 5 minutes, then set aside. Put the flour, baking powder, eggs, sugar and milk in a food processor and blend until smooth. Pour into a large bowl and stir in the banana. Mash the banana into the batter with a potato masher for a minute.

Melt a little of the oil with a cube of butter in a large non-stick frying pan over a medium heat. Wipe around the base of the pan with a thick wad of kitchen paper.

Drop 4 large serving spoonfuls of the banana pancake mixture into the frying pan, spacing them well apart. Cook for 3 minutes, or until the pancakes rise, bubbles appear and the surface appears dry.

Flip the pancakes over with a palette knife and cook them on the other side for 2–3 minutes longer until pale golden brown. Transfer to a heatproof plate and put them into the oven to keep warm while you cook the rest of the pancakes.

Return the frying pan to the heat and add the streaky bacon. Cook for about 3 minutes on each side until golden and crisp, turning once. Add a splash of oil if the rashers begin to stick.

Pile the pancakes onto warmed plates, painting them with the reserved melted butter, and top with the fried bacon. Dribble on a little of the maple syrup and serve the rest separately.

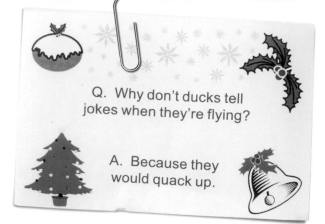

Q. Why don't ducks tell jokes when they're flying?

A. Because they would quack up.

GYPSY TOAST

Gypsy toast, eggy bread, French toast – call it what you like, this is one of those recipes that follows you around. If you fancy eggy bread nothing else will do. When you come in from the pub, when you're camping or when you have nothing in the fridge other than the basics, eggy bread can always put a smile on your face. Use hand-cut white bread if you can – doorstep slices are just right for this. The cream and Parmesan are optional but they really lift the eggy bread to another level.

SERVES 4

3–4 free-range eggs
2 tbsp whole milk
1 tbsp single or double cream (optional)
2 tbsp freshly grated Parmesan cheese
(optional)
4 thick slices of white bread,
hand-cut if possible
sunflower oil
a knob of butter
salt and freshly ground black pepper
(white pepper is also great)

Beat the eggs in a bowl. Add the milk, cream and Parmesan, if using, salt and pepper and beat again briefly.

Pour the eggy mixture into a large dish. Add the slices of bread and leave them to soak for 5 minutes. Then turn the slices over and soak for another 5 minutes. This allows the eggy mix to soak deep into the bread.

Heat the oil and butter in a frying pan over a medium heat. When the butter has melted and the oil is hot, add the slices of bread and cook for 5 minutes per side over a low to medium heat. Serve with bacon and grilled tomatoes or a sausage or two – black pudding would be nice – or just by itself with your saucy preference. The possibilities are endless.

SWEET TREAT

If you fancy a sweet version, add 1 tablespoon of caster sugar and half a teaspoon of cinnamon instead of the cheese and you have French toast. Serve with maple syrup.

REALLY GOOD KEDGEREE

Spicy and delicious, this kedgeree is dead easy to make and perfect for a big family brunch.
Some people love peas in a kedgeree and some don't – it's up to you. It tastes great either way.

SERVES 8–10

475g undyed smoked haddock fillet,
cut in half
2 bay leaves
200g basmati rice, rinsed in cold
water and drained
4 medium free-range eggs
100g frozen peas (optional)
40g butter
1 tbsp sunflower oil
1 medium onion, finely chopped
1 heaped tbsp medium curry powder
3 tbsp double cream
3 tbsp finely chopped fresh parsley
freshly squeezed juice of ½ lemon
black pepper

Place the haddock in a large frying pan, skin side up. Pour over 500ml water, add the bay leaves and bring the water to a gentle simmer. Cook the fish for 8–10 minutes until it is just done and flakes easily. Drain in a colander set over a bowl, reserving the cooking liquor, and discard the bay leaves.

Pour the cooking liquor into a medium saucepan and stir in the rice. Cover with a lid and bring to the boil. Reduce the heat and simmer the rice very gently for 10 minutes. Turn off the heat and leave the rice covered for 3–5 minutes more. By this time it should have absorbed all the fish liquor.

While the rice is cooking, bring some water to the boil in a medium pan. Add the eggs and cook for 8 minutes. Drain them in a sieve under cold running water and when cool enough to handle, peel them carefully and set aside. Cook the peas, if using, in a small pan of boiling water and drain.

Melt the butter with the oil in a large pan and cook the onion over a low heat for 5 minutes until well softened, stirring occasionally. Add the curry powder and cook for another 3 minutes, stirring constantly. Tip the cooked rice into the pan and toss through the onions. Add the peas, cream, parsley and a few twists of ground black pepper and stir well.

Flake the fish into chunky pieces and add these to the pan. Gently stir in the lemon juice and cook for 1–2 minutes. Cut the eggs into quarters and place them on the rice. Cover the pan with a lid and heat through for 2–3 minutes or until the eggs are warm, then serve.

If not serving immediately, tip the kedgeree into a warm dish and dot with a few cubes of butter. Cover with foil and keep warm in a low oven for up to 20 minutes before serving.

HOME-MADE BAGELS
WITH CREAM CHEESE & SMOKED SALMON

Do try making your own bagels – they're a million miles away from the prepacked variety. At first it feels like a leap of faith when you're asked to boil the dough but trust us, the bagels don't fall apart and the boiling is what gives them their special chewy texture.

SERVES 12

500g strong white bread flour
2 tsp dried yeast
1 tsp salt
1 tbsp clear honey
1 free-range egg, beaten
300ml warm water
vegetable oil, for greasing
3–4 tbsp sesame seeds
3–4 tbsp poppy seeds

TO SERVE
smoked salmon
cream cheese

In a food processor, blend the flour, yeast, salt, honey and beaten egg until well combined. Gradually add warm water until the mixture comes together and forms a dough. Then turn the dough out onto a lightly floured work surface and knead lightly until smooth. Place the dough in a bowl, cover and leave in a warm place for at least an hour to rise.

When the dough has risen, turn it out onto a lightly floured work surface and knock back to reduce its volume. Using your hands, divide the dough into 12 portions, roll each one into a ball, then flatten them slightly. Make a hole in the centre of each ball with the handle of a wooden spoon.

Place a sheet of greaseproof paper onto a baking tray and grease lightly with vegetable oil. Place the bagels onto the greaseproof paper, cover them with clingfilm and set aside to rise for 45–50 minutes. Preheat the oven to 230°C/Gas 8.

When the bagels have risen, bring a large pan of water to the boil. Scatter the sesame seeds onto one plate and the poppy seeds onto another. When the water is boiling, lower the bagels into it in batches – use tongs and take care. Poach the bagels for 1–2 minutes, then take them out of the water. While the bagels are still wet, press one side of each into the sesame seeds and the other side into the poppy seeds.

Put the bagels onto the lined baking tray and bake for 10–12 minutes, or until golden brown. Set aside to cool.

To serve, cut the bagels in half and fill with smoked salmon and cream cheese.

EGGS BENEDICT

This is the perfect indulgent breakfast. Home-made hollandaise sauce is much easier to prepare than you may think and beats any kind of shop-bought variety hands down. Use slices of really good ham or smoked salmon, spanking fresh poached eggs and soft English muffins – perfection!

SERVES 6

6 large, very fresh free-range eggs, at room temperature
2 tbsp white wine vinegar
6 English muffins, halved
butter for spreading, at room temperature
6 slices of good ham or smoked salmon
1–2 tbsp finely snipped fresh chives

HOLLANDAISE SAUCE

225g butter, cut into 5–6 chunks
4 tbsp white wine vinegar
1 small shallot or ½ banana shallot, peeled and very finely chopped
10 black peppercorns
1 bay leaf
3 large free-range egg yolks
a pinch of sea salt flakes
a pinch of caster sugar

If you don't want to whisk the egg yolks over simmering water, put the egg yolks, salt, sugar and strained warm vinegar reduction in a food processor, blend briefly, then continue blending while adding the hot butter in a steady stream. It won't be quite as hot as the hob-top version but should still work well.

For perfect poached eggs, see our recipe on page 150, but cook the eggs for only 2 minutes or until the white is just set and the yolk remains very soft. Remove each egg with a slotted spoon as soon as it's ready and plunge into iced water, then remove the eggs and place them on kitchen towel. This process stops the eggs cooking so you can reheat them later. Wash the pan, half fill it with water and set aside until ready to warm the eggs.

To make the hollandaise sauce, melt the butter slowly in a medium pan over a low heat, stirring occasionally. Remove from the heat and pour the butter into a jug. Pour enough water into a medium pan to come a third of the way up the sides. Bring to the boil, then reduce the heat to a simmer.

Put the vinegar, shallot, peppercorns and bay leaf in a small saucepan over a high heat and bring to the boil. Cook for 1–2 minutes or until the liquid reduces to around 2 tablespoons. Keep a close eye on the pan as the liquid can reduce surprisingly quickly. Remove from the heat. Put the egg yolks in a heatproof bowl and place over the pan of simmering water. Whisk the egg yolks with the salt and sugar until pale. Pour the vinegar mixture through a fine sieve onto the yolks and continue whisking until well combined. Slowly add the hot butter in a steady stream, whisking constantly until the sauce is smooth, thick and shiny.

Put the bowl of sauce to one side and whisk occasionally to prevent a skin forming. If it starts to cool too much, pop the bowl back on the warm water and heat through for a minute or so, whisking constantly. Toast the muffin halves and bring the pan of water back to a simmer, ready to reheat the eggs.

Spread the muffins with butter. Put a muffin half on each plate and top with ham or salmon. Using a slotted spoon, drop the cooked eggs into the simmering water and reheat for 1 minute. Remove and gently pat dry with kitchen paper. Place an egg on each muffin and spoon over some hollandaise. Sprinkle with chives and serve, with the other muffin halves on the side.

Nibbles &
telly snacks

HOME-MADE POTATO OR PARSNIP CRISPS

Parsnip or potato, these are easy to make and incredibly tasty.
Treat your guests or make some for yourself to snack on in front of the telly.

MAKES A BIG BOWLFUL

4 large potatoes or parsnips
sunflower oil
sea salt flakes
freshly ground black pepper

Scrub and peel the potatoes. Using the slicing blade on a grater or a swivel-blade vegetable peeler, slice the potatoes into wafer-thin slices. If you have time, drop the potato slices into a bowl of iced water and leave for half an hour – this encourages them to curl and go crispy when you cook them. Heat the oil in a wok or deep fat-fryer to 185°C.

Drain and dry the slices of potatoes thoroughly. Drop the potato slices into the hot oil, a handful at a time. If they stick together while cooking, separate them with a fork. Once they turn pale brown, use a slotted spoon to remove them from the hot oil. Drain on kitchen paper, then season with salt and freshly ground black pepper. Serve immediately, with drinks and a smile.

For parsnip crisps, scrub the parsnips but don't peel them. Slice them lengthways, using the slicing blade on a grater or a swivel-blade vegetable peeler, and continue as for the potato crisps.

You can cook these crisps ahead of time and reheat when your guests arrive. Preheat the oven to 180°C/Gas 4. Spread the cooled cooked crisps on a baking tray and put them into the oven on the top shelf for a couple of minutes. They'll be as crispy as when you first cooked them.

Grate some cheese over the hot potato crisps so it melts and covers the crisps. We suggest some cheddar with chilli or experiment with your favourite cheese.

SPICED MACADAMIA NUTS

These nuts are amazingly delicious and have just the right combination of spice and sweetness. Great with cold lager, wine or a G and T – they won't last long.

SERVES 6

1 tbsp sunflower oil
1 tbsp freshly squeezed lime juice
½ tsp caster sugar
½ tsp garam masala
½ tsp hot chilli powder
½ tsp sea salt flakes
freshly ground black pepper
150g macadamia nuts
1 tbsp clear honey

Preheat the oven to 180°C/Gas 4 and line a baking tray with baking parchment. Using a large metal whisk, beat the sunflower oil and lime juice with the caster sugar until pale. Whisk in the garam masala, chilli, salt and a few twists of freshly ground black pepper.

Drop the nuts into the spiced mixture, stir in the honey and toss everything together until the nuts are evenly covered. Scatter them onto a baking tray in an even layer.

Roast in the preheated oven for 5 minutes, then remove and turn the nuts over. Put them back in the oven for another 8–10 minutes until the nuts have a shiny, golden coating and are no longer sticky. Watch the nuts, as they can burn at the last minute if you're not careful. Cool for a few minutes on the tray as the coating continues to harden. Tip into a bowl and serve warm or cold.

JUMBO CHEESE STRAWS
WITH GORGONZOLA, PARMA HAM & CELERY SEEDS

These are great served with soup or as nibbles with pre-dinner drinks.
Easy to make, but we warn you – make plenty.

MAKES ABOUT 18

1 x 375g pack of puff pastry, defrosted
3 slices of Parma ham
100g Gorgonzola cheese
1 free-range egg, beaten
1 tbsp celery seeds

Roll out the puff pastry into a thin sheet. Cut the Parma ham into strips – keep them thin so that when you bite into the straws you don't pull out a big stringy bit of ham as you tuck in. Preheat the oven to 200°C/Gas 6.

On one half of the pastry lay out the ham, then crumble over the Gorgonzola. Fold the rest of the pastry over the filling, like a sandwich, and roll out thinly again. Trim the edges square. Brush with the beaten egg and sprinkle with celery seeds. Cut into strips of about 1cm wide. Take each strip and twist it into a spiral, then lay it onto a baking tray. Press down the ends slightly to make sure the cheese straws don't uncurl. Bake for about 20 minutes until golden. Leave to cool slightly if you can manage to hold people back!

SAUSAGE ROLLS

These are so simple to make and a complete treat. All your family and friends
will go mad for them. Use good sausages – as plain or fancy as you like.

MAKES ABOUT 18

1 x 375 pack of puff pastry, defrosted
500g good sausages
mixed herbs (optional)
1 free-range egg, beaten

Roll out the pastry into a thin rectangular sheet. Slit the skins of the sausages and squeeze out the meat. Place a strip of sausage meat down the length of the pastry sheet, about 2cm from the edge. Brush the edge of the pastry with some beaten egg, fold it over the sausage meat and seal. Now cut this humongous long sausage roll off from the rest of the pastry and slice into whatever size pieces you fancy, say about 4cm for party size. Repeat until all the pastry and meat are used up.

Preheat the oven to 180°C/Gas 4. Put your sausage rolls onto a baking tray and slash the top of each a couple of times. Brush with beaten egg. Bake for about 20 minutes until golden and cooked through, then leave to cool if you have the willpower!

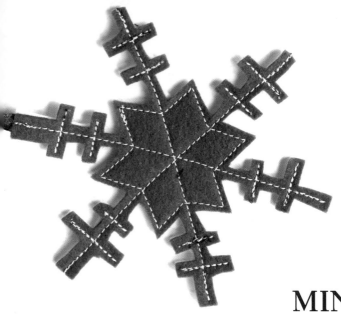

MINI QUICHES

Something to bring out when auntie or the vicar comes to visit. Use your mince pie tin for these and knock them out by the dozen. Our recipe is based on an authentic recipe from Alsace-Lorraine – the home of the quiche – so it's the real deal.

MAKES 12

PASTRY
180g plain flour
100g cold unsalted butter, cut into cubes
2 tsp chopped thyme
50g Parmesan cheese, grated
1 free-range egg yolk
1 tsp ice-cold water

FILLING
3 free-range eggs
150g pancetta, finely diced
250ml crème fraîche
150g Gruyère cheese, grated
freshly ground black pepper

First make the pastry. For best results, keep your hands and kitchen as cool as you can while doing this. Sift the flour into a mixing bowl and rub in the butter until the mixture resembles breadcrumbs. Add the thyme and the Parmesan, then mix in the egg yolk and the water until the dough forms a ball. You may need a tiny bit more water depending on the size of the egg. You can do this in a food processor if you prefer. Wrap the pastry in clingfilm and chill it in the fridge for half an hour.

Preheat the oven to 180°C/Gas 4. Sprinkle some flour on your work surface and roll out the pastry. Using a pastry cutter, cut out discs of pastry of a size to fit your mince pie tin. Think jam tarts – the sides must be high enough to contain the filling. We admit this isn't an easy pastry to work with, but persist – it's worth it.

Grease the tin with a little butter and a sprinkling of flour. Press the pastry discs gently into the tin.

To make the filling, mix all the ingredients, except 50g of the Gruyère, together and stir gently to avoid getting too much air into the mixture. Spoon the filling into the pastry cases and sprinkle the remaining Gruyère over the top. Cook in the preheated oven for about 20 minutes or until the egg mixture has lost its wobble!

CROQUE MONSIEUR

Croque monsieur means something like gentleman's crunch. It's a lovely snack, rich enough
to feel like fun, but with simple flavours to refresh your overloaded taste buds after Christmas.
We love the crunch for brunch with a green salad. If the crunchy fella isn't enough for you, top with
a fried egg to make a croque madame, his other half. She's a teaser – we relish that egg yolk oozing
onto the cheesy, hammy fried duvet of deliciousness.

SERVES 4

75g butter, at room temperature
8 slices of medium-thick white bread
(nothing posh)
1 tbsp plain flour
200ml whole milk
150g Gruyère cheese, grated
2 tsp Dijon mustard
1 tsp Worcestershire sauce
2 free-range egg yolks
4 thick slices of really good ham
2 tbsp vegetable oil

CROQUE MADAME
all of the above
4 free-range eggs

Butter the bread on one side only, using half the butter. Place the slices on a sheet of greaseproof paper, putting 4 slices butter side down and the other 4 butter side up.

Gently warm the remaining butter in a saucepan and mash the flour into it to form a paste. Add the milk, stirring or whisking all the time, to make a thick white sauce and cook until it thickens. Stir in the grated cheese until it melts and add the mustard, Worcestershire sauce and egg yolks. This will make a really thick sauce.

Spread about a tablespoon of the sauce onto the surface of each of the 4 unbuttered sides of the bread. Top with a slice of ham, trimming the meat to fit the bread – a tidy croque is a happy croque. Top each sandwich with the remaining bread, butter side up.

Heat the oil in a frying pan and, when it's at a gentle rumble, fry the croques on both sides until golden. It is the butter sides that are frying and this means that they turn a lovely deep golden colour.

When they are done, remove the sandwiches from the pan and spread the top of each one with another tablespoon of sauce. Pop them under a hot grill until the sauce starts to bubble. Serve with a salad garnish.

For a croque madame, simply top each sandwich with a fried egg before serving.

New Year's
Eve

HAGGIS, CLAPSHOT & WHISKY SAUCE

Haggis, neeps and tatties with a traditional whisky sauce are a must on Hogmanay.
And how about a nice wee dram on the side to warm your cockles?

SERVES 4

1 good haggis
500g floury potatoes
500g turnips (neeps!)
50g butter
2 tbsp chopped fresh chives
sea salt flakes
freshly ground white pepper

WHISKY SAUCE

500ml cream
1 heaped tbsp coarse-grained mustard
1 tbsp Dijon-type smooth mustard
2 tsp whisky
juice of ½ lemon
sea salt flakes
freshly ground black pepper

First cook the haggis. There are a couple of options. The safest way is to wrap it in foil and bake it in its own steam for about 1 hour in a 180°C/Gas 4 oven. Alternatively, simmer the haggis in a pan of boiling water for about 40 minutes per 500g. Watch that the haggis doesn't burst in the pan, but if it does, remove it and heat it through in a frying pan.

To make the clapshot, boil the potatoes and turnips in separate pans until tender. Mash them together with the butter and chives, adding salt and pepper to taste. Some of the more modern recipes suggest adding a little Scottish cheddar as well.

To make the whisky sauce, heat the cream in a saucepan, add as much or little of the mustards as you like, then the whisky. Cook briskly to cook out the alcohol, then season to taste. Whisk in the lemon juice to give the sauce a bit of a zing before serving with the haggis and clapshot.

ROAST VENISON HAUNCH
WITH CHESTNUTS & BACON

A spectacular roast to serve for any festive occasion. Watch the cooking times carefully, as venison is easy to overcook. Ideally, serve rare to medium-rare for juicy, tender meat. Carve the venison into generous slices and serve with creamy mash, green beans and braised red cabbage.

SERVES 8–10

4kg venison haunch on the bone
4 tbsp sunflower oil
150g good-quality rindless smoked streaky bacon rashers, cut into small pieces
200g vacuum-packed chestnuts, sliced
sea salt and freshly ground black pepper
chopped parsley

MARINADE

10 juniper berries
10 black peppercorns
10 cardamom pods
2 star anise
1 medium red onion, peeled and sliced
250ml red wine
150ml gin
freshly squeezed juice and 3 long strips of rind from 1 well-scrubbed orange
4 bushy sprigs of fresh thyme
2 bay leaves

SAUCE

500ml tub of good-quality fresh beef stock
2 tbsp plain flour
2 tbsp redcurrant jelly

To prepare the marinade, lightly crush the spices in a pestle and mortar to release their flavours. Tip them into a large bowl, add the remaining marinade ingredients and mix thoroughly. Add the venison and make sure it is well coated. Cover the bowl with clingfilm and leave the meat to marinate in the fridge for 24–48 hours, turning it 3 or 4 times.

Preheat the oven to 180°C/Gas 4. Drain the venison, setting the marinade aside, then dry the meat and season. Heat 3 tablespoons of the oil in a frying pan and brown the venison on all sides. Put it in a roasting tin and roast in the centre of the oven for 10 minutes per 500g. Add an extra 15 minutes for medium venison and 30 minutes for well-cooked meat.

Pour all the ingredients from the marinade into a large saucepan and add the beef stock. Bring to the boil, then reduce the heat slightly and simmer for 10–15 minutes until the liquid is reduced to around 500ml. Strain through a fine sieve into a jug. Set aside.

Remove the venison from the oven and put it on a warmed serving platter. Cover with foil and a couple of clean, dry tea towels and leave to rest for 20 minutes. Spoon off any excess fat from the roasting tin and place the tin on the hob. Sprinkle over the flour and stir well over a medium heat for 1–2 minutes. Gradually add the stock and marinade mixture, stirring well to scrape up any flavoursome bits from the bottom of the tin. Add the redcurrant jelly and bring to the boil. Reduce the heat slightly and simmer for 5 minutes until the sauce is thickened and glossy, stirring occasionally. Season and add a little extra wine or water if the sauce seems too thick.

Heat a large non-stick frying pan and add the remaining oil. Fry the bacon for 4–5 minutes until crisp. Add the chestnuts and cook for 2 minutes more until hot. Scatter over the parsley, stir quickly, then remove from the heat. Serve with the venison, carved into thick slices, and the hot sauce.

Check the meat with a meat thermometer. Put it into the thickest part of the joint, and take the meat out of the oven at 55°C for rare venison or about 60°C for medium rare.

THAI GREEN CHICKEN CURRY

We love a curry during the festive season and find the spicy hit really refreshing after all the rich food. You may wonder why red chillies in a green curry? They're there because they taste sweeter and add lovely flecks of red to the curry paste, but you can use green ones if you prefer.

SERVES 4

1 tbsp olive oil
6 boneless, skinless chicken thighs, cut into bite-sized pieces
1 x 400ml can of coconut milk
150g mangetout, trimmed
a good handful of fresh basil leaves
a handful of chopped fresh coriander

GREEN CURRY PASTE

2 tsp coriander seeds
3 red chillies, halved and deseeded (more if you like)
2 garlic cloves, peeled
2 lemon grass stalks, trimmed and outer layer removed, then roughly chopped
5 spring onions, trimmed and sliced into short lengths
1 thumb of fresh root ginger, peeled and roughly chopped (about 25g in prepared weight)
6 kaffir lime leaves (dried are fine)
1 large bunch (about 40g) of fresh coriander, trimmed
3 tsp Thai fish sauce (nam pla)
1 tbsp demerara sugar
sea salt flakes
freshly ground black pepper

This makes a fairly mild curry, but if you like your curries spicier, add one or two more chillies.

First make the curry paste. Put the coriander seeds in a small pan and place over a high heat. Cook for 1–2 minutes until they begin to release their fragrance, giving the pan a good shake now and again. Tip the seeds into a pestle and mortar and pound until they are crushed to a powder.

Transfer to a food processor and add the chillies, garlic, lemon grass, spring onions, ginger, lime leaves, coriander, fish sauce and sugar. Blitz until all the ingredients are very finely chopped and form a thick paste. You may need to push the mixture down a couple of times with a spatula. Season with a good pinch of salt and plenty of ground black pepper and whizz for a few seconds more.

Heat the oil in a large non-stick frying pan or wok and stir fry the chicken for 1–2 minutes over a medium-high heat until it is no longer pink. Add the curry paste and cook with the chicken for 2–3 minutes longer. Pour over the coconut milk, bring to a simmer and cook for 2 minutes. Add the mangetout and simmer for 2 minutes longer, stirring occasionally. Don't let the chicken overcook. Stir in the basil and coriander leaves and ladle the curry into bowls. Serve with some freshly cooked jasmine rice.

CITRUS-CRUSTED CHICKEN BREASTS

Serve up this wonderfully tangy chicken dish with some potato latkes
for a tasty New Year's Eve supper that all the family will love.

SERVES 6

2 garlic cloves, crushed
2 tsp chopped fresh thyme
1 tsp sea salt flakes
2 tsp cracked black pepper
zest of 2 limes
juice of 1 lime
6 tbsp olive oil
6 chicken breasts
100g smoked streaky bacon rashers,
cut into lardons

Using a pestle and mortar, grind the garlic, thyme, salt, pepper and lime zest with the lime juice and 2 tablespoons of the olive oil to make a paste. Set aside.

Slash the skin of the chicken breasts in 3 or 4 places. Heat the rest of the olive oil in a frying pan and sauté the bacon until crispy to release the fat. Add the chicken breasts and sauté them on both sides – you just want to seal them and give them a little colour. Don't cook them for too long or they will get tough. Preheat the oven to 180°C/Gas 4.

Put the chicken breasts to a roasting tray, skin side up, and spread them with the lime paste. Roast for about 20 minutes until cooked, basting frequently. Check that the breasts are done, but be careful not to overcook, as you want the meat to be nice and juicy. Leave to rest for 10 minutes before serving with the delicious citrusy cooking juices.

POTATO LATKES

These are a nice alternative to rosti and can be made in advance
and warmed up in the oven when you're nearly ready to eat.

MAKES 6 BIG ONES

1kg floury potatoes, such as
King Edwards or Maris Pipers, peeled
2 onions, peeled and chopped
2 large free-range eggs, beaten
2 tsp salt
1 tsp freshly ground black pepper
vegetable oil, for shallow frying

Grate the potatoes and onions onto a clean tea towel – you need to work quickly or the potatoes will go brown. Spread the grated veg out, then roll up the tea towel and squeeze out the liquid. Tip the mixture into a bowl, add the beaten egg and seasoning and stir well.

Heat the vegetable oil in a frying pan. Add spoonfuls of the mixture to make rounds of about 6cm across. Cook the latkes for 5 minutes, then turn them over and fry for 5 minutes more until they are golden and cooked through.

EXTRA-SPECIAL LAMB BIRYANI

This is a one-pot wonder for a crowd – just the thing for a New Year's Eve party – and although it takes a while, once it's done you can relax. You can prepare the saffron milk and cook the lamb well ahead of time, then spread the lamb in the dish it's going to be baked in, cover and chill for up to 24 hours. (The saffron milk can also be left to soak in the fridge.) Roughly one and a half hours before serving, bring the lamb to room temperature, half cook the rice and scatter it over the lamb. Bake as in the recipe below but for a bit longer, 45–50 minutes, until the lamb is piping hot and the rice is tender.

**SERVES 6 GENEROUSLY
or 8–10 AS PART OF A
LARGER MEAL/BUFFET**

100ml whole milk
1 small sachet of saffron (0.4g)
or 1 heaped tsp
4 medium onions, peeled
4 garlic cloves, peeled
1 thumb-sized piece of fresh root
ginger, peeled and roughly chopped
1 plump fresh red chilli, deseeded and
roughly chopped (more if you like)
50g flaked almonds
6 cloves
2 tsp cumin seeds
2 tsp coriander seeds
¼ cinnamon stick
10 cardamom pods
2 tsp sea salt flakes,
plus extra to season
½ nutmeg, finely grated
½ tsp freshly ground black pepper
plus extra to season
900g–1kg lamb shoulder meat
sunflower oil
200ml full-fat natural yoghurt
2 bay leaves
50g sultanas
350g basmati rice
40g butter
3 large free-range eggs
4–5 tbsp roughly chopped fresh
coriander, plus extra to garnish

Pour the milk into a small pan, add the saffron threads and heat gently for 2–3 minutes without boiling. Remove from the heat and set aside for 2–3 hours or overnight.

Roughly chop 2 of the onions and put them in a food processor with the garlic, ginger, chilli and half the flaked almonds. Add 50ml cold water and blend to a paste. Put the cloves, cumin and coriander seeds in a pestle and mortar, or an electric spice grinder, with the cinnamon, seeds from the cardamom pods and a teaspoon of salt. Pound or grind until as powdery as possible. Add the grated nutmeg, sprinkle with black pepper and tip into the onion paste. Blitz quickly until all the ingredients are combined.

Trim the lamb of any hard fat and cut into bite-sized pieces. Heat 2 tablespoons of oil in a frying pan, season the lamb with salt and ground black pepper, then fry in 2 or 3 batches until browned on all sides. Tip into a large heavy-based saucepan as each batch is browned. Add more oil as needed.

Pour another 3 tablespoons of oil into the same frying pan and cook the onion paste until lightly browned, stirring often. Add a little water if the paste begins to stick. Tip into the pan with the lamb. Stir in the yoghurt and bay leaves. Place the pan over a low heat and stir in 300ml water. Bring to a gentle simmer, cover and cook over a low heat for 45–60 minutes or until the lamb is tender, stirring occasionally.

Cut the remaining 2 onions in half and slice thinly. Heat 2 tablespoons of oil in a large non-stick frying pan and cook the onions for 6–8 minutes until softened and golden brown, stirring often. Drain on kitchen paper. Put the rest of the almonds in the pan and cook for 2–3 minutes until lightly toasted. Turn often so they don't burn. Stir the sultanas into the almonds, then tip into a heatproof bowl and leave to cool.

This makes a fairly mild curry. If you like something a bit hotter, add an extra chilli or two.

When the lamb is tender, remove the lid and increase the heat. Boil the sauce until reduced and thick, stirring often. This will probably take around 10 minutes, depending on how long the lamb has been cooking for. Add a little more seasoning if necessary.

Meanwhile, preheat the oven to 180°C/Gas 4. Half fill a large pan with water, add a teaspoon of salt and bring to the boil. Put the rice in a sieve and rinse under plenty of cold water. Stir the rice into the hot water and return to the boil. Cook for 5 minutes, then drain well. Pile the meat and sauce into a large, fairly deep ovenproof dish. Spoon over the part-cooked rice and drizzle with the soaked saffron threads and milk. Dot with the butter, scatter with half the fried onions, then cover the dish with 2 layers of tightly fitting foil. Bake for 30 minutes.

While the lamb and rice is in the oven, hard-boil the eggs for 10 minutes. Shell the eggs and cut into quarters. Put the reserved fried onions in a small frying pan and heat through over a low heat. Take the dish of lamb and rice out of the oven and remove the foil. Gently mix in the chopped coriander, then garnish with the eggs, hot onions, toasted almonds and sultanas. Add a few fresh coriander leaves and serve.

CRANBERRY & LIME VODKA JELLY SHOTS

These shots will start any party with a bang. Only a little gelatine is used, so the shots can be slurped with ease. If you have fairly narrow shot glasses, you may need teaspoons to reach the jelly right at the bottom.

SERVES 12–15

3 sheets of leaf gelatine
375ml cranberry juice drink
50g caster sugar
150ml vodka
finely squeezed juice of ½ lime

Put the gelatine sheets in a bowl and cover them with cold water. Leave to soften for 5 minutes. Pour the cranberry juice drink into a medium saucepan, add the sugar and heat gently until lukewarm. Remove from the heat.

Lift the gelatine from the water and squeeze it to remove as much liquid as possible. Drop the gelatine into the warm cranberry juice and stir until completely dissolved. If the juice isn't warm enough to melt the gelatine, put it back on the heat for a couple of minutes more.

Stir the vodka and lime juice into the cranberry mixture and pour into a jug. Place your shot glasses on a tray and pour the mixture into them. Cover loosely with clingfilm and chill for several hours until lightly set.

GIN & TONIC SORBET

SERVES 6

300g caster sugar
finely grated zest of
2 well-scrubbed limes
150ml freshly squeezed lime juice
(about 6 fresh limes in total)
150ml freshly squeezed lemon juice
(about 4 fresh lemons)
100ml tonic water
6 good slugs of gin
lime slices, to decorate

Put the sugar and lime zest in a pan with 200ml of water and slowly bring to the boil, stirring occasionally. Boil for 5 minutes, then remove from the heat. Strain the juices through a fine sieve into a bowl. Strain the sugar syrup into the same bowl, add the tonic and stir well. Leave to cool.

Pour the mixture into an ice cream maker and churn until it has a soft sorbet-like consistency. This may take over an hour. Tip into a freezer-proof container and freeze for at least 6 hours before serving. Scoop the sorbet into glass tumblers and pour over a good slug of gin. Decorate with slices of lime if you like – see the picture on page 23.

New Year's
Day
∾

CHICKEN LIVER PARFAIT
WITH CRANBERRY BUTTER

This smooth, creamy pâté turns cheap chicken livers into something special and is perfect
as a starter or light lunch. Top with tangy cranberry butter for an extra burst of flavour.

SERVES 6

200g butter
1 medium banana shallot
or ½ small onion, finely chopped
1 bushy sprig of thyme
1 bay leaf
2 garlic cloves, finely chopped
a good pinch of ground nutmeg
a good pinch of ground allspice
500g chicken livers, trimmed
50ml brandy
50ml Madeira
3 tbsp double cream
sunflower oil, for greasing
sea salt flakes
freshly ground black pepper

CRANBERRY BUTTER
100g butter
6 tbsp cranberry sauce (choose a bright
red one if possible – fresh cranberry
sauce will give the best colour)

Melt 50g of the butter in a medium pan and gently fry the
shallot with the thyme and bay leaf until well softened but
not coloured, stirring regularly. Add the garlic, nutmeg and
allspice and cook for 1 minute more, stirring.

Drop the chicken livers into the pan and cook over a high heat
for 2–3 minutes or until lightly browned and hot. Cut one of
the largest livers in half to check – it should look pale pink
inside. Pour the brandy and Madeira into the pan and boil
hard for 1–2 minutes or until almost all the liquid evaporates.

Remove the pan from the heat and discard the thyme and
bay leaf. Tip the chicken liver mixture into a food processor
and season with plenty of salt and pepper. Melt the remaining
150g butter in a small pan over a low heat. Blend the chicken
liver mixture for a minute, then remove the lid and push the
mixture down with a spatula. With the motor running, slowly
pour the melted butter onto the liver, then add the double
cream and blend for a few seconds more.

Transfer the mixture to a fine sieve placed over a bowl and
press it through firmly, using a ladle to push the mixture
through the tiny holes. Grease 6 x 100ml ramekins or small
dishes with sunflower oil and divide the mixture between them.

To make the cranberry butter, melt the butter in a small pan
over a very low heat. Remove from the hob and pour into a
measuring jug. Spoon off any foam that rises to the surface
and leave to stand for a few minutes to allow the milk solids
to sink to the bottom of the jug. When the butter looks clear,
tip it back into the pan and stir in the cranberry sauce. Warm
together gently for a few minutes, stirring occasionally until the
sauce melts. Leave to cool for 10 minutes.

Spoon a little sauce onto each ramekin and leave to cool.
Cover with clingfilm and chill for 2 or 3 hours or overnight
until set. Eat within 3 days.

To serve, take the parfaits out of the fridge 20 minutes before eating. Put the ramekins on small plates with toasted brioche or granary bread.

BASIL & WHISKY SMOKED SCALLOP & PRAWN KEBABS
WITH BURNT ORANGE & SESAME DRESSING

This is the only good kind of smoking, but take care with your smoke alarm!
You'll need a handful of barbecue woodchips and 2 wooden skewers for this recipe.

SERVES 2

1 tbsp malt whisky
1 handful of chopped basil, leaves and stalks
4 king scallops
6 raw tiger prawns, shelled
lamb's lettuce or other salad
sea salt flakes

BURNT ORANGE & SESAME DRESSING
1 orange, cut in half
2 tbsp olive oil
1 tsp sesame oil
2 tsp light soy sauce
1 tsp clear honey
zest of ½ orange

Soak the woodchips for 30 minutes and squeeze them dry. Soak 2 wooden skewers in water for at least 10 minutes. Place a pad of 2 sheets of foil inside a wok, then put the woodchips on top, drizzle on the whisky and add the basil.

Clean the scallops, remove the orange roes and set them aside. Cut each scallop in half. Take the 2 wooden skewers and thread on pieces of scallop, alternating them with prawns. Place the skewers on an oiled rack over the wok.

Cover the wok with a lid, seal any gaps with more foil and place over a moderate heat for 10 minutes. Turn off the heat and leave the shellfish to smoke and infuse for another 5 minutes. While this is happening, prepare the dressing.

Place the halved orange, cut side down, in a dry frying pan over a high heat for 3 minutes until caramelised (burnt!). Squeeze the juice from the burnt orange into a bowl and add the olive oil, sesame oil, soy sauce, honey and orange zest. Mix well and set aside.

Bring a small pan of salted water to the boil. Add the scallop roes and poach them for 1 minute, then dry them on some kitchen paper and set aside.

To serve, place the kebabs on top of a bed of salad. Drizzle on the dressing. Slice the roes finely and arrange them over the salad – the bright orange slices look fantastic against the green leaves. Season with sea salt to taste.

SALMON PASTILLAS
WITH SALAD & SALMON ROE

This is one of our favourite dishes. The salmon roe pop
in your mouth as you eat the scrumptious pastillas.

SERVES 4

4 sheets of filo pastry.
4 x 75g pieces of salmon fillet, trimmed
to about the size of a thin matchbox
12 marinated anchovy fillets
(boquerones)
4 tsp soured cream
4 tsp chopped fresh dill
1 tsp lemon juice
1 free-range egg, beaten
vegetable oil, for shallow frying
salad leaves (we recommend
rocket and watercress)
1 x jar of salmon roe
sea salt flakes
freshly ground black pepper

DRESSING
2 tbsp olive oil
1 tbsp white wine vinegar
2 tsp honey
a pinch of salt

Lay a sheet of filo pastry on a floured work surface. Cut a
slit into one of the salmon portions and lay it on the edge of
the pastry. Tuck 3 anchovies, a teaspoon of sour cream and
a teaspoon of fresh dill into the salmon and close it up, then
sprinkle the salmon with a little lemon juice, black pepper and
sea salt. Roll the salmon and filo into a neat parcel, sealing it
with beaten egg. Repeat to make 3 more parcels and brush
them all with beaten egg.

Heat the oil in a frying pan and shallow fry the pastillas until
golden. Be careful not to overcook them – the salmon should
still be juicy.

Meanwhile, wash the salad leaves and mix together the oil,
vinegar, honey and salt to make the dressing. Put some salad
leaves onto the plates and dress, then scatter some salmon roe
on top of the leaves. Add a beautiful golden salmon pastilla to
each plate.

GUINNESS, BEEF & CHESTNUT CASSEROLE
WITH LEEK COLCANNON

We cooked this for Michael Flatley's Lord of the Dance team at Sunderland Empire.
By the time they'd eaten this lot, it was more like Lord of the Stroll than dance!

SERVES 6

2 heaped tbsp plain flour
1 tsp sea salt flakes
1 tsp freshly ground black pepper
1kg stewing steak, cut into chunks
2 tbsp vegetable oil
3 large onions, peeled and sliced
1 tbsp tomato paste
8 carrots, peeled and cut into discs
2 celery sticks, chopped
500ml beef stock
250ml Guinness
1 tsp caraway seeds
1 tbsp raisins
20 chestnuts, cooked, peeled and sliced
2 tbsp chopped parsley

LEEK COLCANNON

1kg good floury spuds, peeled
and cut into big chunks
250ml milk
500g leeks, washed and cut into rounds
1 huge knob of butter
1 tbsp double cream
sea salt flakes
white pepper

Preheat the oven to 150°C/Gas 2. Place the flour in a plastic bag, add the salt and pepper and give it a good shake. Add the chunks of stewing steak and shake again until all the beef chunks are nicely covered in the seasoned flour.

Heat the oil in a frying pan and brown the meat in batches, then transfer the meat to a casserole dish. In the same frying pan, cook the onions until translucent, add the tomato paste and cook for 2 minutes. Add the onions to the casserole with the carrots, celery, beef stock, Guinness, caraway seeds and raisins. Mix well, then cover the pan with a lid.

Cook in the preheated oven for 2 hours until the meat is tender. Add the chestnuts and cook for a further 30 minutes. If the casserole seems too liquid, put it on the stove top and cook with the lid off for 5 minutes or so until the liquid has reduced. Sprinkle with parsley and serve with leek colcannon.

LEEK COLCANNON

Add the potatoes to a big pan of boiling water and poach gently until the potatoes are soft – poaching in simmering water rather than boiling gives you better mash. Heat the milk in a separate pan, add the leeks and poach them for about 5 minutes until cooked. Mash the potatoes, add the butter and cream, then stir in the leeks. Add a little of the milk from the leeks, but don't make the mixture too sloppy. Season to taste with the sea salt and white pepper.

SLOW-ROASTED PORK BELLY
WITH FRUITY MULLED CIDER CABBAGE

Belly pork is cheap but delicious and this is one of our favourite meals.
The fruity, spicy cabbage is the perfect accompaniment.

SERVES 8–10

1 whole pork belly, boned
3 star anise
6 cloves
2 Granny Smith apples, peeled, cored and sliced
2 large Navel oranges, thickly sliced
200ml organic medium cider
sea salt flakes

GARNISH
salt-roasted almonds (optional)

MULLED CIDER CABBAGE
1 small red cabbage
25g butter
1 large onion, finely sliced
2 star anise
1 cinnamon stick
¼ tsp freshly grated nutmeg
1 bay leaf
8 tbsp cider
2 tbsp light muscovado sugar
2 tbsp redcurrant jelly
sea salt flakes
freshly ground black pepper

Score the skin of the pork with a very sharp knife – or ask your butcher to do this for you when you buy the meat. Pour boiling water over the skin – this will help the crackling crackle – then dry it and rub generously with sea salt.

Preheat the oven to 180°C/Gas 4. Put the star anise, cloves, sliced apples, oranges and cider into a roasting tin. Place the pork on top, cover with foil and roast for 1½ hours. Remove the foil, turn the oven down to 150°C/Gas 2 and continue cooking the pork for another 1½ hours. Take the meat out of the oven and leave it to rest for 15 minutes.

Turn the pork skin side down and cut the joint into squares. Then serve a portion, skin side up this time, onto each plate with some cabbage. Garnish with salt-roasted almonds if you like and add a spoonful of the cooking juices.

MULLED CIDER CABBAGE
Finely slice the cabbage, chucking out the core and any tough pieces. Use a pan that has a tight-fitting lid and is large enough to hold all the cabbage. Melt the butter in the pan and cook the onion, uncovered, for 5 minutes until it is soft but not browned.

Add the star anise, cinnamon stick, nutmeg and bay leaf, then the cabbage, cider and sugar. Stir until everything is thoroughly mixed and the sugar has dissolved. Season generously. Bring to the boil, then cover the pan tightly and simmer for about 1 hour, stirring occasionally, until the cabbage is very tender and the liquid has evaporated. Stir in the redcurrant jelly and allow it to melt. Remove the star anise and cinnamon stick before serving.

LOVE IN A TRANSIT

Or if you insist – coq au vin! Ask your butcher to joint your chicken if you don't want to do it yourself, or buy chicken thighs, legs or part-boned breasts. Coq au vin doesn't normally contain tomatoes, but we think our version is the better for them, as they simmer down to make a rich, tasty sauce. Serve with creamy mashed potatoes and green beans, garnished with freshly chopped parsley.

SERVES 4

2–3 tbsp sunflower oil or mild olive oil
1 medium-large chicken (about 1.8kg), jointed into 8 portions
125g unsmoked streaky bacon rashers, rinds removed, cut into 2cm slices
1 medium onion, peeled and finely diced
2 large garlic cloves, peeled and finely chopped
50ml brandy
750ml red wine
1 x 400g can of chopped tomatoes
2 bay leaves
2–3 bushy sprigs of fresh thyme or ½ tsp dried thyme
16 small shallots, peeled
200g baby button mushrooms, wiped
chopped parsley
sea salt flakes
freshly ground black pepper

Heat a tablespoon of the oil in a large non-stick frying pan. Season the chicken all over with a little salt and plenty of pepper, then brown it in the frying pan over a medium to high heat, turning once. Do this in a few batches so you don't overcrowd the pan and transfer each batch to a flameproof casserole dish. When all the chicken is browned, add the bacon to the pan and cook for a couple of minutes until it begins to crisp, turning often. Scatter the bacon over the chicken. Add the diced onion to the pan and cook over a fairly low heat for 4–5 minutes until golden brown, stirring often. Add a touch more oil if you need it. Add the garlic for the last minute or so, then tip everything into the pan with the chicken.

Deglaze the pan with the brandy, stirring well to remove as much of the tasty sediment from the pan as possible. Add half the red wine and bubble for a few seconds more. Pour the hot brandy and wine mixture, and the rest of the wine, over the chicken and add the tomatoes and herbs. Bring to a gentle simmer, cover loosely with a lid and cook for 30 minutes over a fairly low heat.

Meanwhile, prepare the shallots and mushrooms. Heat a tablespoon of oil in a clean frying pan and fry the shallots until lightly browned, stirring occasionally. Add the mushrooms to the pan and cook them with the shallots for a couple of minutes until golden brown, turning every now and then. Stir the shallots and mushrooms into the casserole dish after the chicken has been cooking for 30 minutes. Cover loosely again and simmer gently for a further 30–45 minutes or so, until the chicken is tender and the onions are softened.

Using a slotted spoon, transfer the chicken and vegetables to a large bowl. Return the sauce to the hob and bring it to the boil. Cook the sauce for 5 minutes until it has thickened, stirring regularly. If you leave the chicken in the pan, you risk toughening it. When the sauce has reduced enough to coat, put everything back in the casserole and warm it through. Sprinkle with parsley before serving.

LUSCIOUS CHESTNUT & CHOCOLATE ROULADE

This is richer than a Premier League footballer and makes your chocolate log look like a mere hors d'oeuvre! Well worth the effort and hugely impressive.

SERVES 8

softened butter, for greasing
6 large eggs, separated
150g caster sugar
50g cocoa powder

FILLING
150g plain dark chocolate, broken into squares
300ml double cream
300g chestnut purée (from a can)
40g caster sugar

TOPPING
50g plain dark chocolate, broken into squares
50g white chocolate, broken into squares
1 tsp icing sugar

Preheat the oven to 180°C/Gas 4. Line a 23 x 33cm Swiss roll tin with baking parchment, grease with a little butter and set aside. Put the egg yolks and sugar in a large bowl and whisk with an electric whisk until thick and creamy. Sift the cocoa powder over the egg mixture and whisk in thoroughly. Wash and dry the beaters. Whisk the egg whites in a clean bowl until stiff but not dry. Fold a third of the egg whites into the cocoa mixture, then gently fold in the rest until evenly distributed. Pour into the prepared tin and spread gently with a spatula.

Bake in the centre of the oven for 20–25 minutes until risen and just beginning to shrink away from the sides of the tin. Remove from the oven, loosen the edges with a round-bladed knife and leave to stand for a few minutes. The cake will sink down into the tin. Place a piece of baking parchment on the work surface, turn the cake onto the parchment and leave to cool completely.

To make the filling, melt the chocolate with 150ml of the cream in a non-stick pan over a low heat, stirring occasionally until smooth. Remove from the heat. Put the chestnut purée in a food processor with the sugar. With the motor running, slowly add the melted chocolate and cream and blend until smooth and light. Trim the edges off the cooled chocolate sponge and gently spread with the chestnut mixture.

Whip the rest of the cream until soft peaks form and spread it over the chestnut and chocolate filling. Using the parchment paper to help you, roll the cake up from one of the short sides and carefully lift it onto a wire rack.

To make the topping, melt the dark and white chocolate in 2 heatproof bowls over pans of simmering water until smooth, stirring occasionally. Using a teaspoon, drizzle the melted chocolate over the roulade and leave to set for at least 30 minutes. Chill until ready to serve. Remove from the fridge 30 minutes before serving and dust with a little sifted icing sugar.

Twelfth
Night

BANGING APPLE, CIDER & ONION SOUP

Forget your fancy French onion soup – this'll stick to your ribs, we promise you.

SERVES 10 AS A STARTER OR 6 FOR LUNCH

75g butter
1kg onions, peeled and sliced
2 large leeks, washed and sliced
2 eating apples, peeled and sliced
2 large potatoes, peeled and diced
150ml cider
1 litre chicken or vegetable stock
3 bay leaves
1 sprig of thyme
200g Gruyère cheese, grated
2 heaped tbsp chopped chives
grated nutmeg to taste
sea salt flakes
freshly ground black pepper

Melt the butter in a large pan, add the onions, leeks and apples and sweat until translucent (10–15 minutes should do it). Keep stirring regularly so the leeks and onions don't brown. A brown onion is an unhappy onion, especially in a white soup. Add the potatoes and stir.

Pour in the cider, bring to the boil and boil for a couple of minutes to reduce the liquid. Add the stock, bay leaves, seasoning and thyme, cover and cook for 25 minutes until all the veggies are cooked through. Remove the thyme and bay leaves. Blitz half the soup in a blender until smooth and return to the lumpy broth in the pan. This gives a lovely texture.

To serve, ladle the soup into bowls and add a handful of cheese, some chopped chives and a pinch of nutmeg to taste.

SALMON COULIBIAC

This salmon dish comes from Russia and is fantastic hot or cold for a Twelfth Night feast. Serve with hollandaise (see page 159), dill sauce (see page 10) or melted butter. It looks great and tastes better.

SERVES 12–15

1 salmon, filleted into 2 sides, skinned and pin boned
½ fish stock cube
100g long-grain rice
1 free-range egg
200g cooked peeled prawns
1 tbsp chopped fresh dill
1 tbsp chopped flat-leaf parsley
1 dsrtsp chopped chives
50g chopped mushrooms
finely grated zest of 1 lemon
1 tsp lemon juice
2 x 375g packets of puff pastry
100g baby spinach leaves
1 free-range egg, beaten
sea salt flakes
freshly ground black pepper

Check that all the little pin bones have been removed from the salmon. Dissolve the stock cube in a jug of boiling water and use the liquid to cook the rice according to the instructions on the packet. Leave to cool.

Preheat the oven to 180°C/Gas 4. In a mixing bowl, fold together the cold rice, egg, prawns, dill, parsley, chives, mushrooms, lemon zest and juice to make the stuffing. Season to taste and work everything together well with your hands.

Roll out the puff pastry into 2 rectangular sheets, slightly bigger than your salmon, to make the top and bottom of the coulibiac parcel.

Put a layer of spinach leaves over the bottom sheet of pastry and place a fillet of salmon on top. Spread the stuffing over the salmon – it will be about 2cm thick. Place the other fillet of fish on top to make a sandwich.

Wrap the rest of the spinach leaves around the sides of the salmon and over the big sandwich and put the other sheet of puff pastry on top. Brush the edges with beaten egg to help seal them and make a tidy parcel. Trim off any excess pastry and use it to craft a pastry salmon, highland scene or whatever takes your fancy to put on top of the coulibiac.

Carefully lift the parcel onto a greased baking tray and cut a couple of steam holes into the top. Brush with beaten egg and cook in the preheated oven for 25–30 minutes until golden. Wonderful served hot or cold with some salad.

CHICKEN THIGHS
WITH PARSLEY, THYME & LEMON STUFFING

Chicken thighs are cheap but tasty and this stuffing makes them into a really special meal. Ask your butcher to bone the meat for you and make sure you have some cocktail sticks for securing the thighs.

SERVES 4

2 tbsp olive oil
1 small onion, finely chopped
2 garlic cloves, crushed
75g fresh white breadcrumbs
1 tbsp chopped fresh parsley
2 tsp thyme leaves
zest and juice of ½ lemon
1 free-range egg yolk
6 boned chicken thighs, skin intact
a few knobs of butter
sea salt flakes
freshly ground black pepper

First make the stuffing. Heat the oil in a frying pan and sweat the onion and garlic until translucent. Mix the breadcrumbs, parsley, thyme, zest and juice in a bowl until well combined, then add the cooked onion and garlic. Stir in the egg yolk and season to taste.

Preheat the oven to 180°C/Gas 4. Lay a chicken thigh out flat and place a portion of the stuffing in the middle. Roll it up and secure it with a cocktail stick. Stuff the remaining thighs in the same way, put them all in a roasting tin and dot with knobs of butter. Roast for 40 minutes until the thighs are cooked through and golden.

HASSELBACK OR
HEDGEHOG POTATOES

These are great – a bit fancy and long forgotten. If you like crispy potatoes with a bit of style, then these are the ones for you.

SERVES 6

6 good medium-sized potatoes
100g butter, melted
fine sea salt and ground white pepper

Put a potato into a tablespoon and cut lots of slices down through the potato – the edges of the spoon stop you cutting all the way through. Cut all the potatoes in the same way and put them in water until you are ready to cook them. This preparation can be done ahead of time.

Preheat the oven to 180°C/Gas 4. Dry the potatoes, season and paint them with melted butter. Bake the potatoes in the preheated oven for about 45 minutes or so until crispy. Baste with more melted butter about half way through.

OUR SPECIAL WINTER FISH PIE

After aeons of research, we have produced our version of a perennial favourite – fish pie.

SERVES 6

1.5kg good old potatoes (King Edwards,
Maris Pipers, Estimas or similar)
a big knob of butter
white pepper
100g Gruyère cheese, grated
1 litre fish stock (can use cubes)
4 tbsp dry vermouth
1 onion, peeled and roughly chopped
1 small bulb of fennel, cored and chopped
1 small carrot, peeled and chopped
1 small celery stick, chopped
1 bay leaf
a pinch of saffron
750g white fish (haddock, hake, sea bass,
halibut… that sort of thing)
250g smoked haddock
200g salmon
120g raw prawns, unshelled
75g unsalted butter
75g plain flour
150ml whole milk
a large handful of finely chopped parsley
150ml double cream
4 hard-boiled free-range eggs
125g spinach, blanched and drained
25g ciabatta breadcrumbs
25g Parmesan cheese, grated
sea salt flakes
freshly ground black pepper

First cook the potatoes – poaching gently in simmering water rather than boiling gives best results – then mash them with a big knob of butter and add salt and white pepper to taste. Fold in the Gruyère and set aside.

Pour the fish stock into a pan and add the vermouth, onion, fennel, carrot, celery, bay leaf and saffron. Bring to the boil and simmer for 5 minutes. Carefully add the fish and prawns to this broth and poach for 3 minutes, then gently lift them out and set aside.

Strain the soggy vegetables and the herbs from the broth and discard. Bring the broth back to the boil and simmer until reduced by half.

Preheat the oven to 180°/Gas 4. To make the parsley sauce, melt the 75g of butter in a pan and mix in the flour to form a paste. Pour in the reduced broth, a little at a time, and keep whisking until smooth. Add the milk and the parsley, bring to the boil and simmer for 10 minutes to cook out the flour. Add the double cream and season to taste.

Flake the fish, discarding any skin and bones, and peel the prawns. Lay the fish and prawns in a buttered casserole dish and pour in about half the parsley sauce to cover the fish. Save the rest to use as a pouring sauce to serve with the pie.

Slice the hard-boiled eggs and lay them on top of the sauce, followed by the spinach. Cover with the cold mashed potatoes in a rough and ready fashion. Mix the ciabatta crumbs with the Parmesan and sprinkle on top. Bake in the preheated oven until the pie is piping hot and the topping is golden brown.

Perfect served with broad beans, pancetta and shallots (see page 116).

ROAST PORK HOCKS
WITH POTATO SALAD

If you like crackling and super-juicy pork, you'll love this recipe. It's cheap and easy to make too, so just right after your Christmas splurge. Note: the mayonnaise contains raw eggs.

SERVES 6–8

3–4 pork hocks
2–3 tbsp mild olive or sunflower oil
1 bunch of watercress, trimmed, washed and drained
olive oil
squeeze of lemon juice
sea salt flakes
freshly ground black pepper
chutneys and pickles, to serve

POTATO SALAD

1kg new potatoes, well scrubbed
3 large free-range egg yolks
2 tbsp white wine vinegar
1 tbsp Dijon mustard
1 tsp caster sugar
½ tsp sea salt flakes
freshly ground black pepper
300ml sunflower oil
200ml tub crème fraîche
1 bunch of spring onions, trimmed and finely sliced
1 tsp caraway seeds (optional)

Preheat the oven to 160°C/Gas 3. Rub the pork hocks all over with the oil and season with salt and pepper. Place in a roasting tin and cook in the centre of the oven for 2 hours. Increase the oven temperature to 190°C/Gas 5 and bake the pork for a further 50–60 minutes or until the rind is very crisp and the meat is tender. A knife inserted into the meat from the thick end should slide in easily and the pork should readily pull away from the bone.

When the pork hocks are cooked, pull off the crisp crackling and break it into chunky pieces, then pull the meat away from the bones. Transfer the crackling and pork meat to a warmed serving platter. Toss the watercress with a little olive oil, lemon juice and plenty of seasoning. Use to garnish the meat. Serve with the creamy potato salad, pickles and chutney.

POTATO SALAD

Put the potatoes in a large pan of salted water and bring to the boil. Reduce the heat to a fast simmer and cook the potatoes for 18–20 minutes, or until tender but not breaking apart. Rinse in a colander under cold running water for a couple of minutes, then leave to drain thoroughly. Cut the potatoes in half, or into thick slices if large.

To make the creamy mayonnaise, put the egg yolks, vinegar, mustard and sugar in a food processor. Season with the salt and some ground black pepper. Blitz until smooth, then with the motor running, gradually add the oil and blend until smooth and thick. Add the crème fraîche and 2–3 tablespoons of cold water. Blend for a few seconds more, adding more water if necessary, until the sauce has a soft, dropping consistency.

Tip the potatoes into a bowl and mix with the mayonnaise and spring onions. Check the seasoning. Scatter the caraway seeds into a dry frying pan and toast over a medium heat for 2–3 minutes, shaking the pan regularly. Sprinkle the seeds over the salad and add a little black pepper before serving.

BEEF BOURGUIGNON

It's worth getting well-hung meat from the butcher for this recipe. Supermarket meat is often too lean and becomes dry rather than succulent during the long cooking process. If you want to get ahead, cook up to the point at which the onions and mushrooms are added, then leave to cool before covering and chilling for up to two days – or freeze if you prefer. Warm through gently on the hob until bubbling, then add the freshly fried button onions and mushrooms, and cook for the remaining time in the oven.

SERVES 6–8

1.5kg good braising steak
4–5 tbsp sunflower oil
200g smoked bacon lardons or smoked streaky bacon, cut into 2cm pieces
1 large onion, peeled and finely chopped
2 garlic cloves, peeled and crushed
1 x 75cl bottle of red wine
2 tbsp tomato purée
1 beef stock cube
2 large bay leaves
3 bushy sprigs of thyme
450g button onions, or roughly 24 baby onions
25g butter
300g button chestnut mushrooms, wiped and halved or quartered if large
2 tbsp cornflour, mixed with 2 tbsp cold water
freshly chopped parsley, to serve
sea salt flakes
freshly ground black pepper

Cut the steak into chunky pieces, each about 5cm, trimming off any hard fat or sinew as you go. Season the beef well with salt and pepper. Heat 2 tablespoons of the oil in a large frying pan. Fry the beef in 2 or 3 batches over a medium-high heat until nicely browned on all sides, turning every now and then, and adding more oil if necessary. As soon as the beef is browned, transfer it to a large flameproof casserole dish. Preheat the oven to 160°C/Gas 3.

Add a little more oil to the pan in which the beef was browned and fry the bacon for a couple of minutes until the fat crisps and browns. Tip the bacon onto the beef. Add a touch more oil to the pan and fry the chopped onion over a low heat for 5–6 minutes, stirring often, until softened. Stir the garlic into the pan and cook for 1 minute more. Add the onion and garlic to the casserole dish with the meat and pour over the wine. Stir in the tomato purée and 150ml of cold water. Crumble over the stock cube, add the herbs and bring to a simmer. Stir well, cover with a lid and transfer to the oven. Cook for 1½–1¾ hours or until the beef is almost completely tender.

While the beef is cooking, peel the button onions. A few minutes before the beef is ready, melt half the butter in a large non-stick frying pan with a little oil and fry the onions over a medium-low heat for about 5 minutes or until golden on all sides. Tip into a bowl. Add the mushrooms to the pan and cook for 2–3 minutes over a fairly high heat until golden, turning often.

Remove the casserole from the oven and stir in the cornflour mixture, followed by the onions and mushrooms. Return to the oven and cook for 30–45 minutes more, or until the beef is meltingly tender. The sauce should coat the back of a spoon, but if it seems too thin, add a little more cornflour, blended with some cold water, and cook for a few minutes on the hob. Sprinkle with freshly chopped parsley and serve.

Button onions are fiddly to peel so here's what we do. Put them in a heatproof bowl and cover with just-boiled water. Leave for 5 minutes, then drain. When they are cool enough to handle, trim off the root close to the end and peel off the skin.

KINGY CAKE

This cake's proper name is galette des rois, or the kings' cake, but we like to call it Kingy cake. It's a traditional Twelfth Night dish, made to celebrate the visit of the Three Kings to the baby Jesus on Epiphany, and it's really quick to make and bake. You don't have to use jam, but it does taste extra delicious with it – a bit like a cheat's Bakewell pudding.

SERVES 8

500g ready-made puff pastry
125g butter, softened
125g caster sugar
1 tsp vanilla extract or 1 tbsp brandy
2 medium free-range eggs
125g ground almonds
2 tbsp plain flour, plus extra for rolling
4 tbsp raspberry jam (optional)

Cut the pastry in half and roll out each piece on a lightly floured surface until large enough to cut out a 25cm round. Use a dinner plate as a template if you like. Put the pastry circles on flat baking trays and chill for 30 minutes.

Preheat the oven to 200°C/Gas 6. Cream the butter and sugar with the vanilla extract, or brandy, in a food processor until light and fluffy. Lightly beat the eggs, setting aside 2 tablespoons in a small bowl for brushing the pastry later.

With the processor on, add the remaining beaten egg to the sugar and butter mixture and blend until smooth. You may need to remove the lid and push the mixture down a couple of times with a spatula. Add the almonds and flour, then process again until well combined.

Remove the pastry from the fridge and spread one of the rounds with the jam, if using, to within 4cm of the edge. Spoon the almond mixture on top and spread it gently over the jam. Brush the pastry edge with a little of the reserved egg and place the other round on top.

Press the edges firmly to seal, then 'knock up' with a sharp, knife to help separate the layers so they puff up while the cake is cooking. To do this, hold the knife at right angles to the edges and gently tap them together. Score the surface with a sharp knife, then brush with the beaten egg you set aside. Bake in the centre of the oven for 30–35 minutes or until puffed up and golden brown. Remove from the oven and serve warm or cold in wedges.

Recipes

BREAKFAST & BRUNCH

American banana pancakes with streaky bacon 153
Bagels, cream cheese & smoked salmon 158
Corned beef hash & poached eggs
    with jumbo pretzels 150
Croque Madame 171
Croque Monsieur 171
Eggs Benedict 159
Gypsy toast 154
Really good kedgeree 157
Smoked salmon, dill & ricotta fritters with
    lime-seared scallops 149

CAKES & BREADS

Banging banana, walnut & sultana bread 60
Chocolate yule log 67
Christmas cake 18
Cinnamon swirls 146
Hairy Bikers' stollen 63
Home-made marzipan 72
Kingy cake (galette des rois) 217
Panettone 38
Panforte 40

DRINKS

Best-ever mulled wine 86
Christmas pudding vodka 30
Creamy egg nog 86
Royal gin fizz 86
Sloe gin 30

FISH

Basil & whisky smoked scallop & prawn kebabs with
    burnt orange & sesame dressing 190
Christmas gravlax with dill, treacle & cumin 13
Lemon & parsley roasted salmon with champagne
    & chive sauce 100
Our special winter fish pie 211
Salmon coulibiac 206
Salmon pastilla with salad & salmon roe 191

Si's mussels with cognac & cream 79
Traditional gravlax with dill & mustard sauce 10

MEAT

Beef bourguignon 214
Extra-special lamb biryani 182
Guinness, beef & chestnut casserole
    with leek colcannon 195
Haggis, clapshot & whisky sauce 174
Loin of venison in a sloe gin & blackberry glaze
    with candied shallots 53
Roast loin of pork with prune & apple stuffing 102
Roast pork hocks with potato salad 212
Roast venison haunch with chestnuts & bacon 176
Slow-roasted pork belly with fruity mulled cider cabbage 196
Spiced beef with root vegetables 49
Traditional honey-glazed gammon 50

NIBBLES

Home-made parsnip crisps 164
Home-made potato crisps 164
Jumbo cheese straws with Gorgonzola, Parma ham
    & celery seeds 168
Jumbo pretzels 150
Mini quiches 169
Sausage rolls 168
Spiced macadamia nuts 165

PATES & TERRINES

Chicken liver parfait with cranberry butter 188
Coarse country terrine 76
Potted smoked mackerel pâté 96
Transylvanian terrine 85

PICKLES

Last-minute Christmas chutney 29
Pickled onions 14
Pickled pears 14

POULTRY

Chicken thighs with parsley, thyme & lemon stuffing *209*
Christmas turkey with two stuffings *108*
Citrus-crusted chicken breasts *181*
Cold turkey & ham pie with cranberry topping *130*
Dave's spatchcocked duck *80*
Festive duck breast with lemon & thyme polenta *46*
Goose risotto *133*
Love in a transit (coq au vin) *199*
Roast goose with ginger & orange stuffing *106*
Stuffed chicken breasts with rosti potato cakes *82*
Thai green chicken curry *179*
Turkey & ham pancakes *139*
Turkey curry *136*
Turkey sandwich with chips & gravy *138*
Warm pigeon breast salad with lime
     marmalade dressing *134*

PUDDINGS & SWEET SAUCES

Blackcurrant & cassis sorbet *21*
Brandy cream *120*
Brandy sauce *120*
Christmas panna cotta *122*
Christmas pudding fondants *54*
Christmas pudding ice cream *20*
Classic brandy butter *120*
Coffee cardamom zabaglione with affogato *89*
Cranberry & lime vodka jelly shots *185*
Cranberry, date & macadamia pudding
     with butterscotch sauce *125*
Easiest-ever mango sorbet *21*
Gin & tonic sorbet *185*
Luscious chestnut & chocolate roulade *200*
Old-fashioned mince pies with an orange crust *64*
Traditional Christmas pudding *17*
White chocolate & sour cherry cheesecake *70*

SAVOURY SAUCES

Bread sauce *119*
Cranberry, kumquat & port sauce *112*
Dill & mustard sauce *10*

Gravy *104, 106, 108*
Hollandaise sauce *159*

SOUPS

Banging apple, cider & onion soup *205*
Chestnut, roasted butternut squash & Bramley apple soup *45*
Jerusalem artichoke soup with bacon & parsley croutons *95*
Turkey & vegetable soup *129*

SWEETS & BISCUITS

Brandy snaps with ginger cream & chocolate *141*
Candied peel *37*
Chocolate orange & cranberry biscotti *36*
Chocolate orange-crisp truffles *32*
Creamy Christmas fudge *33*
Lebkuchen *69*

VEGETABLES, SIDES & SALADS

Black pudding mash *116*
Broad beans with pancetta & shallots *116*
Brussels sprouts *112*
Candied shallots *53*
Chipolatas wrapped in bacon *119*
Chips *138*
Crispy roast potatoes *112*
Dates wrapped in bacon *119*
Glazed carrots *113*
Goat cheese salad with honey & mustard dressing *99*
Hasselback potatoes *209*
Leek colcannon *195*
Mulled cider cabbage *196*
Mustard mash *116*
Nut & spinach roast with wild mushroom gravy *104*
Potato latkes *181*
Potato rosti cakes *82*
Potato salad *212*
Roast parsnips *113*
Roast garlic mash *116*
Sage & onion mash *116*

Index

Acknowledgments

We owe a huge debt of gratitude to the following people. First, thanks to all our friends and colleagues at Orion who have helped us and worked so hard to produce this beautiful book: our expert editors, Susanna Abbott and Amanda Harris; the lovely Michael Dover; artistic goddess Lucie Stericker; and love to our good friend and colleague, publicist Angela McMahon.

We thank Jinny Johnson, queen of the English language, Kate Barr for her fabulous design, and Cristian Barnett, our photographer, whose pictures make us hungry and who manages even to make us two look presentable.

Enormous thanks and respect to Sammy-Jo Squire, Nikki Morgan and Justine Pattinson for their culinary expertise.

We would also like to thank Paul Kelly for the turkey info, Michael Jones for his cheesey knowledge and our old drinking pal Jeff Pickthall for his beer tips.

Thanks, too, to both our families for putting up with us obsessing about turkey and chestnuts, while other families were celebrating Easter.

Finally, huge thanks to Santa and all his elves and fairies, without whose help and Christmas spirit none of this would have been possible.

Paul Kelly's KellyBronze turkeys are available from:
Kelly Turkey Farms, Danbury, Essex CM3 4EP
Tel 01245 223581
www.kellyturkeys.co.uk

Michael Jones sells cheese at:
The Cheeseboard, 26 Royal Hill, London SE10 8RT
Tel: 020 8305 0401
www.cheese-board.co.uk

For more information on beer, see Jeff Pickthall's blog:
http://jeffpickthall.blogspot.com